Frequently-Asked Questions in
Christian Theology

Frequently-Asked Questions in Christian Theology

William H. Harrison

mowbray

Continuum

The Tower Building	80 Maiden Lane
11 York Road	Suite 704
London SE1 7NX	New York, NY 10038

www.continuumbooks.com

First published 2008

British Library Cataloguing-in-Publication Data

A catalogue record for this book is available from the British Library.

ISBN 978 19062 8616 3

Typeset by YHT Ltd, London
Printed and bound by Cromwell Press, Wiltshire

To

Charles Hefling,

who teaches me to think and love,

and

Rita,

who teaches me to love and think

Table of Contents

How to Read this Book   ix

1 Thinking Theologically   1
   What is the Bible?   1
   Where does the Bible come from?   2
   How should we read the Bible?   5
   What sorts of questions do scholars ask about the
   Bible?   7
   What use is human intelligence?   10
   What use is tradition?   12
   Why do Christian positions on moral issues change?   13
   What is a doctrine?   16
   Why does Christian thinking change?   22
   How does theology relate to the physical sciences?   25
   Can we know whether a religious claim is true or
   not?   28
   What sort of language do we use to talk about God?   31

2 God   35
   Who is the Christian God?   35
   Why does the Bible show God doing things which
   appear to be evil?   37
   How did the Christian understanding of God
   develop?   41
   What do we mean when we speak of God as
   "eternal"?   44
   Why do we believe in the Trinity?   47

Table of Contents

Who is God the Father? 51
Who is Jesus Christ? 53
1. Introduction: Jesus and the Trinity 53
2. What is the significance of Jesus's birth? 55
3. How can Jesus be fully divine and fully human? 58
4. How does Jesus's life serve the Reign of God? 60
5. Why did Jesus die? 66
6. What is the significance of Jesus's resurrection? 72
7. What is the significance of Jesus's ascension? 75
Who is the Holy Spirit? 77

3 Salvation 83
What is salvation? 83
What is God's grace? 85
What is eternal life? 86
What are justification and sanctification? 89
What is redemption? 93
What is freedom? 96
What is heaven? 98
What is the kingdom of God? 99
What do we mean when we talk about "Christ's
return"? 103
Can non-Christians be saved? 107
What happens to people who reject God? 111

4 The Church 116
What is the church? 116
Why go to church? 120
Why join the church? 122

5 Worship and Prayer 127
Why do we pray? 127
What is a sacrament? 131
What is baptism? 134

Table of Contents

What is the eucharist?   138
What are icons and why do people use them?   142
Why do we celebrate the Christian year?   145

6 The Problem of Evil   153
   What is the good?   153
   What is evil?   156
   What is original sin?   159
   What is the Devil?   161
   Can there be a just war?   165

Conclusion: What is the gospel?   170
   What is the gospel?   170

How to Read this Book

This volume is intended for people who have little or no formal training in theology. It arises out of a conversation which I have had with many different people (both Christian and non-Christian) since I became a theologian. There are some occupations which tend to be real conversation-killers. Being a theologian is not one of them; the moment that I mention my work, I get to hear about the personal belief-system of each person in the group and get tossed a great many difficult questions at the same time. As it happens, this is what I do for fun, so I have no complaints. On the other hand, the conversation tends to be pretty much the same, so my wife just sits back with a knowing smile on her lips and observes as we make our way through the usual discussion. Partly at her urging, I have opted to put all of this material into a book. At the very least, if the conversation is cut short for any reason (as it often is), then I can sell a book and explain that the rest of what I want to say is in there.

This volume, then, is intended to be accessible to the general reader. It does not, however, fall into the category of a "sermon" or "popular spirituality" or any of the "feel-good" oriented books on the store shelf. Instead, this is intended to be genuine, solid introductory theology. Much of what I have taught seminary students is in here. Thus, you may find some parts challenging to understand. You may also find them difficult to accept, perhaps because some of what I say differs from what you have previously been taught. Consequently, you will need to approach this book as a conversation partner. Be prepared to take some time over it; I think that you will find your efforts rewarded, even if only because your views are clarified by being compared with what I say.

How to Read this Book

In order to make that sort of conversation possible, I have structured this book in a question-and-answer format. The questions tend to be short and blunt, which is the kind that people usually address to me. The answers are brief, usually under five pages. This means that you need not read the book from start to finish initially; you may wish to look up some of your more pressing questions in the "Table of Contents" and turn to those first. On the other hand, you may find that approach only partially helpful, since some answers assume that you have read earlier parts of the book.

The other advantage of the question-and-answer system, and the real reason for my use of it, is that you can read the book in short portions, then leave it and meditate on what you have learned. This is a disastrous approach to the usual sort of volume of systematic theology. Long (and often dense) chapters do not lend themselves to reading on the bus, where I hope that this book will appear. You can read one or two questions and then reflect upon them while doing other things. This is a book for people who live in today's busy society, but want to enter into the rich world of Christian theology.

Such a book is likely to inspire scepticism within the halls of academic theology, however, and for a very good reason. The disadvantage of the brief question-and-answer approach is that subtleties, complexities and disagreements tend to receive little "airtime" or get lost altogether. That is a fair criticism. I do not pretend to outline every viewpoint on every question, much less resolve every debate, in this one small volume. If you become involved in the discussion and find that you want to argue with my conclusions, then I congratulate you and strongly encourage you to take up the study of theology. Nothing would give me greater pleasure than to know that one person found my work stimulating enough to investigate the field of theology further. This book is not the last word on anything. I hope only that it is the starting word on some very important things for some interested people.

There is one last thing which I ought to say about my style of writing. Many people will expect such a book to be filled with biblical references and quotations. There certainly are some discussions of biblical passages and some references – a great many, in fact. On the whole, however, I tend to find the habit of constant referencing to be off-putting; it interferes with my ability to read. Rarely do I find that people actually pursue the references; commonly, when ardent students do so, the passages are found to need significant interpretation in order to yield the meanings intended by the original footnote in the book being studied. In short, I think that authors are much better advised to explain themselves in the first place, rather than relying on simple biblical quotation to back up a viewpoint. Therefore, you may find noticeably fewer biblical references than you expect in this book. To those who ordinarily read Christian books with Bible in hand, my apologies.

I hope that you will elect to continue with your reading. Please, enjoy yourself. If there is no joy to be found in something, then you are manifestly doing the wrong thing and ought to stop immediately.

Blessings,

William H. Harrison

Thinking Theologically

1

What is the Bible?

The Bible is often the first part of Christianity that people encounter. Christians are often called "people of the Book." When I was a child, there was a Gideon Bible in every North American hotel room. Indeed, the Gideon Bible Society even showed up in our school rooms to hand out New Testaments; often, they were covered in red leather; always, they were in the King James Version, with the words ascribed to Jesus written in red. This points to what most North Americans would give as the answer to our question: "The Bible is a book." Some would add that it is broken into two parts, usually labelled "Old Testament" and "New Testament." Simple enough, it would seem.

However, closer examination of the question, even at this basic level, reveals that the answer must be more complex than it seems.

All Christians read a collection of literature called the Bible. In the standard Protestant Bible, there are 66 "books" (some are poems, some letters – a whole variety of things). However, the Roman Catholic Bible, the Greek Bible (used by some Orthodox churches) and the Slavonic Bible (used by a variety of Eastern Christians) contain other material; these Bibles are not identical to each other or to the Protestant Bible. On top of all this, both Protestant and Roman Catholic Bibles exist in a variety of translations, each reflecting a somewhat different understanding of the Hebrew and Greek texts which serve as sources. In other words, we cannot even start with an agreement that there is one, given, book which constitutes "the" Bible.

Is this a problem? Well, not necessarily. It is a difficulty if you believe that God wrote every word in the Bible personally, by injecting it into the heads and taking control of the hands of the human authors. This view became popular in the 17th century, as modern notions of what constitutes a "fact" came into being. Such an approach has been used to support a contemporary kind of "literalism," in which every word of the text is deemed to be straight from God. Many people will put this position beyond argument by insisting that this is true of the "original texts" only; since we cannot be sure what the original texts looked like, there can be no dispute about such a stance. However, since we lack the original texts, the argument is irrelevant – what difference does it make if the original texts are divinely dictated, when we do not have them and could not be certain that they were the first even if we had some likely candidates? Evidently, we must account for a human role in the formation of whichever selection of texts we call the Bible.

The dispute about the role of God in forming the Bible does raise an important question for us, though. Commonly, the Bible is called "the Word of God." Is this appropriate? What does it mean?

The Bible does not call itself "God's Word." It saves that title for Jesus and for some particular examples of God speaking, whether directly or through people. We can, however, call the Bible "God's Word" if we are very careful about explaining our meaning. The Bible is a collection of stories about people encountering God, hearing God speak, and trying to understand God. The Bible is particularly important to us, and different from any other book, because it tells the story of Jesus. Jesus is God's self-communication to the world, the one who tells us who God is and what God is doing. That makes the Bible into God's Word for us. In it, we meet the God who brings us into being, loves us and cares for us. Thus, we hear God speaking about Godself in the Bible, in spite of all the complexities around reading it.

Where does the Bible come from?

Many Christians would respond to this question with a simple: "from God." That is, indeed, part of the Christian answer, but only part. It hides the complicated human history of involvement with the text.

When you first encountered the Bible, where did you find it? How did it get to you? Most likely, the church was somehow involved in your discovery of the Bible. You may have learned about it in a church, whether at a Sunday School or in some kind of service. Alternatively, you might have been introduced to it by someone at school or work, or you may simply have pulled it out of a drawer in a hotel room. However that happened, the church was involved. The church has always been in this position, because the Bible is, in some important ways, the church's book. Only because the church values the Bible – reading it, publishing it and sharing it – has it occupied a central place in world history and the lives of many people.

The church's involvement does not stop at this. The Bible was not written in any of the languages in which we ordinarily read it. The first part, known as the "Old Testament" or "Hebrew Scriptures," was written in Hebrew. The second part, usually called the "New Testament," was written in Greek and contains a smattering of Aramaic phrases. The Bibles which we read are translations from these original languages. Many translations are available, because the act of translating is complex. Sometimes, translators must guess at the meaning of a word or phrase in the original language, employing all of their training to make a reasonable attempt to understand the intended meaning. Where such guessing is necessary, translators will differ about what word or phrase constitutes the most likely possibility. Further complicating the task is the difference among languages. Often, there is no direct parallel between ancient Greek and Hebrew and a contemporary language such as modern English. The Greek word *logos* is usually translated as "word," but *logos* means much more; it implies "reason," in the sense of rationality, which is understood to be the ordering force of the cosmos (universe). So much is intended by *logos* that no English equivalent can be found. We must be satisfied with partial equivalence.

One of the ways that we make up for the inadequacy of translation is by teaching people about the Bible. This is another of the ways in which the church is involved with the text. All but the most unusual of Bible teachers have learned much of what they know about the Bible and its meanings from other teachers. Many clergy, including nearly all of those in leadership in mainstream churches, have attended seminaries or colleges to learn about Christianity and the Bible. The church has formed them and given them a role in helping you to understand the Bible. Those teachers have learned from the church and they are serving the church by teaching you. In other words, churchpeople are at the centre of the community which interprets the Bible to the world; people rarely meet the Bible without meeting the church also.

This follows logically from the Bible's origins. We can discern God's work in helping to bring the Bible into existence. Concretely, however, the church's early leaders are the ones who chose to retain the Hebrew Scriptures; they composed the gospels, letters and other material found in the New Testament; and they assembled all of this into one collection which came to be called the Bible. The early church decided what would count as Christian Scripture.

Moreover, in a series of meetings of bishops (called "church councils"), the church made decisions about which interpretations of the text would be deemed acceptable and which would not. Later in this volume, you will be able to read about the development of doctrines (teachings) about the Trinity and Jesus Christ. These doctrines were not created arbitrarily; they were responses to questions which arose about the church's worship and message, and about the Bible. People discovered that the text could be understood in different ways. The church, which assembled the Bible and called it "sacred," insisted that some meanings which people had drawn from it did not accord with the message which the church believed and taught. Consequently, some rules of interpretation were laid down in the creeds of the church.

The church, therefore, has been intimately involved with the biblical text since before it was deemed to be sacred Scripture. Christians who call themselves "Evangelical" tend to emphasize reading the Bible and making a personal decision for God as a consequence of what the Bible teaches. They are right to insist that the religious decision is an intensely personal one. However, we must all remember that "personal" does not imply "purely individual," in this case. There cannot be a wholly individual decision about the God whom we meet in the Bible, because when we read the Bible we hear the church speaking. The Bible has formed the church over the ages, forcing the church continually to rethink its ideas and actions. Similarly, the church has formed the Bible, by bringing it into existence, establishing rules for its interpretation, translating it and teaching about it. The relationship is a mutual one and a continuing one, as we struggle to discern the meaning and significance of the Bible's words for us, today.

How should we read the Bible?

We read the Bible because it changes our lives, teaching us about God and what God is doing in creation. We always need to keep this overriding principle in mind as we try to decide how to approach this often difficult book. Indeed, the Bible can be tough to read. It is a collection of material of many kinds. Moreover, it is an ancient book, so it often follows different rules from modern literature. On top of all this, the Bible reflects all of human life, which is complex and not always pretty.

At the most basic level, the Bible is where we encounter the heart of the Christian story. The majority of our Bible talks about the relationship between God and the Hebrew people. These stories display the Hebrew conviction that God is at work in their history, loving them and caring for them even when the Hebrew people are not faithful to God. We accept this overall conviction, even when we cannot agree with the biblical authors about actions attributed to God.

The Christian Bible centres on the story of Jesus Christ, which is the story of God taking on humanity, suffering the worst that humans could throw at anyone (including a miserable and dis-honourable death), and overcoming these things. This is the announcement that God gives a life that overcomes all kinds of death. The Bible also shows us something of how the early church responded to this news, with bewilderment and failure, as well as great joy and rapid growth.

Christian thinkers have always recognized that there are

difficulties with reading the text in a simple, "literal" (as we use the word), way. Historical details are not always absolutely consistent in the text; for example, John's Gospel has Jesus arrested one day earlier than the other Gospels – compare John 19:31 with Matthew 26:17. Some events could not have happened as recounted. For example, the sun is once described as standing still in the sky (Joshua 10:13); however, we know that the sun does not move relative to us and the earth would be destroyed by even a very brief stop in its rotations, so the story is not likely to be accurate physics. Moreover, there are portions, such as the early chapters of Genesis, which are written in the language of myth and symbol, rather than that of history (as we understand the term).

Consequently, scholars develop technical ways to approach these stories, in order to understand what they were intended to mean for their original audiences and how such stories might be useful for us. Learning about the history of the text and the people who composed it helps us to know their intention. We can read the stories with a deeper sense of what was meant in the contexts for which the stories were originally composed. In addition, studying how stories have worked among different people helps us to understand why these stories were shaped in this way. Different cultures use stories differently; the First Nations people of North America, for example, speak their stories and use them in a poetic fashion to help in understanding the world, whereas much of modern North American thinking appears in written and critically-debated texts.

We need to hear the Bible in church and pray with it. However, we also need to study it and make use of commentaries and other scholarly resources if it is to come alive for us in the 21st century. We are intensely aware of the historical and cultural distance between us and the biblical text. The only way in which we can, at least partly, overcome that distance is to employ the research of scholars. Their ongoing efforts to elicit meaning from the Bible enable the book to be something more to us than a dead pad of paper with black marks on it. We can see the similarities between our lives and the lives of people long-dead, and find the meaning which God intends for us, here and now.

What sorts of questions do scholars ask about the Bible?

There are two basic approaches which scholars take to reading the Bible. Usually, the first is what is called "historical-critical." It involves raising questions about the origins and development of the text, from its roots in oral and written form to the final edition that we read. This type of study is sometimes called "diachronic," because it considers the text in at least two time periods – first, a period of origin or development, and second, the present form. There are a variety of methods by which diachronic study is undertaken; the most common are: source-criticism, form-criticism and redaction-criticism. We will address these in a bit more detail, but let us first mention the other scholarly approach to biblical research.

The second type of study is called "narrative-critical." Often, it will use the results of historical research as stepping-stones. However, the focus of narrative study is the text in its current form, which is why it is called "synchronic." This form of investigation tries to identify clues in the story that will help us to understand the intended meanings of the text as we have it.

The examination of a portion of the Bible (scholars call an identifiable piece of the text a "pericope") might follow these steps:

First, one might ask about the origins of the text, which is the purpose of source-criticism. Does this text use other sources which can be identified? An example of this can be found in the Gospels of Matthew and Luke, which appear to share some reliance on the Gospel of Mark. Because Mark is briefer and is likely used elsewhere, it is probably the oldest of these three Gospels. Seeing the differences in the ways in which Marcan material is used in Matthew and Luke can be revealing about the intentions of the people who composed these two Gospels. A more complicated application of source-criticism can be found in the study of some other material that Matthew and Luke share. This material, largely in the form of "sayings" of Jesus, is commonly held to have come from a text which we do not have, called "Q" (from the German *Quelle*, which means "source"). Again, the work of identifying these shared pieces and demonstrating similarities and differences in usage can help to show what the people who composed Matthew and Luke knew and what they wanted to say with the knowledge that they were passing on.

A second, and related, step in an examination of a text is finding pieces (again, "pericopes") which follow existing conventions for particular forms (form-criticism). In other words, there are books in the Bible that we know to be letters, intended both for particular persons and for groups. When we write letters, we use identifiable styles. For example, we often begin letters with the phrase "Dear ... " Someone who reads the letter must recognize that the word "dear" does not necessarily imply, in this case, that the recipient is a highly valued friend of the sender (which is what "dear" means in some other contexts). "Dear" is nothing more than a stylistic convention; it appears in letters to complete strangers. In order to understand the letters in the Bible, we need to know that they are letters and what portions of them are, in the sense which we have discussed, conventional. The same goes for hymns, prayers, treaties and other forms of speech or text that might be used when composing another text. Form-criticism is the set of techniques by which scholars identify such pericopes and identify conventions, departures from convention and content that is unique to the particular letter (or hymn, sermon, prayer ...) under examination.

This brings us to the third sort of question that scholars address to biblical texts. When someone composing a piece of writing uses other sources and forms, shaping them into something new, that person functions as an editor. Redaction criticism (from the German *Redaktion*, which means "editing") is the name given to the work of examining the ways in which editors have affected the text. This work naturally flows out of source and form study, because it focuses upon how the editor has modified the material to suit its new context. Sometimes, scholars will trace the work of successive editors, as in the case of Isaiah, which likely consists of two or three texts fitted together. What do the portions composed by each editor appear to say? How are those statements modified by being placed beside each other in one large text? Redaction-criticism investigates these stages in the development of a text and the shifts of meaning which a text undergoes each time it is newly edited.

All of these approaches yield information that can be used in the fourth type of study which scholars undertake: narrative-criticism. This is an examination of the text in its final form, in an attempt to understand how the various words and phrases work together to create a meaningful story (or letter, sermon, etc....). This approach is similar to the ways in which the average person reads the Bible; indeed, some narrative scholars discuss precisely that: the ways in which ordinary people study the Bible in particular historical contexts (while under oppression, for example). This sort of study can shed light on how people might have encountered biblical texts in days gone by, as well as being helpful advice for using the Bible today.

There is an important difference between scholarly, critical reading and ordinary, reflective reading, however. A narrative-critical reading tries to approach the text in a fresh, open way, but with the benefits of careful historical study and a rich understanding of the language and culture of the people who composed the text. Thus, Adele Berlin dedicates a sizeable portion of a classic book in this field to discussing the impact that the use of the word "behold" (*hinneh*, in Hebrew) has on some Hebrew stories in the Bible (*Poetics and Interpretation of Biblical Narrative*, Sheffield: Almond Press, 1983).

The result of all this work is that we have a great variety of literature about the Bible. Approaching the "Biblical Studies" section in a theological library can be a bit daunting. It is worthwhile, though, even for someone without training. Many books about the Bible have been written so that they are accessible for the average person. Looking at commentaries is often helpful for simple, in-home Bible study. A careful look at different commentaries will usually help in selecting one that is scholarly, yet still matches your reading level. Try to find one which discusses other research on the section of the Bible which you wish to study. That is often a good indicator of whether you are getting a serious, scholarly book, rather than a simply popular (commonly preachy) serving of one person's off-beat views.

Because this volume is a discussion of theology, rather than a biblical commentary, I will not call your attention to my reliance on these various techniques of scholarship in the course of discussion. You will need to remember, however, that my reading of biblical texts is shaped by critical study. This will affect my conclusions and may require you to think differently about the Bible as you develop the capacity to think theologically in the contemporary world.

What use is human intelligence?

When we talk about religion, we commonly ignore human intelligence. Some people prefer to speak about emotional or spiritual experiences. They love to talk about visions, dreams and other sorts of encounters with a different reality in which humans are largely passive recipients of some gift. Speaking about a vision often makes us feel special, somehow individually blessed. Other people tend to speak of divine revelation, in which God hands us the truth and we need only to live it out. This approach has the virtue of simplicity and trust-worthiness. It carefully limits the kind and amount of effort that participation in religion demands of us.

Visions can be helpful and God does speak to us, but we must not ignore the role that our minds play in religious life. Without our minds, things which happen to us are merely that: things which happen. Experience, as such, is just stuff that happens to us and of which we are aware. As Charles Hefling points out, "Pure experience is like pure water: it may exist, but samples of it are extremely rare."[1] Experience is almost always *experience as understood*. Those emotions, visions, dreams and other kinds of encounters with the Other all end up being interpreted. We use our minds to understand them. Unless our intelligence comes into play, we do not even have anything to tell other people about.

The same thing is true about anything else to which we wish to

---

1. Charles Hefling, *Why Doctrines?* (Chestnut Hill (MA): Lonergan Institute at Boston College, 2000), 12.

refer. When we speak about the world as reflecting the glory of God (or as showing evidence of evil), we are talking about the world as we understand it. When we talk about encountering God (or failing to encounter God) in the stories of the Bible, we are talking about the Bible as we understand it. Seeing, hearing and reading are all acts of intelligence.

In short, our minds work as mediators. The information that we use at any level higher than the merely physical and automatic is processed by our intellect. This is a good thing. God has given us reason to help us gather information, formulate understanding, check the accuracy of our conclusions, and make decisions on the basis of our understanding.

We do not do this alone. We could not make any sense of the black marks on paper which make up a Bible if we had not been trained to read, both in the non-technical sense of elementary education and in the more technical sense of Christian formation. That is part of what the church is for. It helps us to understand who God is and what God does. In other words, the church uses its intelligence to speak to everyone's intelligence. Life in the church is an ongoing conversation about God and the world and that is only possible because we have minds.

The church functions as an interpretive community, helping us to understand both the world and the Christian message, while considering how these two should meet. It has done so for nearly two millennia, which makes the church's history an important part of its thinking, as we shall see in further sections.

This interaction among various sources of data, on the one hand, and our intelligence and the mind of the church, on the other, means that Christian education is very important. The world is a complicated place; our lives are complex and demanding. Christian thinking cannot be simplistic or it will be unhelpful – perhaps even dangerous. We need to use all the resources of our minds and hearts to understand God, our world, and the meeting places between them.

We have already seen an example of the importance of human intellect to the work of theology. Any kind of Bible reading involves activity of the mind; careful, scholarly reading requires trained intelligence. Moreover, contemporary understandings of the Bible and its meanings are dependent upon past thinking. The intellectual work of the church is ongoing and central to Christian life. That is why we now turn to a discussion of "tradition."

What use is tradition?

We live in a world that is endlessly fascinated with things which are new and different. People seek out the newest bestsellers and the latest gadgets. Progress is everything and faster is always better. Computers are obsolete almost as soon as they hit the stores; businesses commonly replace them every 4 years or so. Information stored away only 25 years ago is becoming inaccessible to us because the software and hardware used for its preservation have vanished.

In a world like this, claiming some value for the past seems pointless. The past is a foreign country, and an irrelevant one, isn't it? Besides, we know more than the people of 2000 years ago, don't we? Well, not necessarily. Besides, everything that we know builds on what they knew.

Christian thinking is a conversation that occurs over time. The doctrine of the Trinity, which is the belief that God is one unity of three persons, is not *in* the Bible. Nor is the doctrine of Christ, which asserts that Jesus the Christ is both fully human and fully God. Both of these understandings developed through centuries of early church conversation and continue to develop as we ask and answer questions about them. Both of these teachings (which is what a "doctrine" is) are a product of the church's effort to understand what God teaches us about Godself. We need to know the history of that conversation in order to understand what the teachings mean.

We have all had the experience of being quoted out of context. We know that one consequence of this is that our words come to mean something different from what was originally intended. Sometimes, the new meaning is richer than the original, showing us that our insight was deeper than we thought at the time. At other times, however, we find ourselves in trouble, because our words are made to mean something harmful or disgusting. Then we attempt to explain ourselves, trying to demonstrate that we did not mean what is being heard. Only when we clarify the history of our words can we show people what we really meant to say.

Tradition works like that. Simply giving a person a Bible and saying that this is what the church means to say is unhelpful; treated like this, the Bible is merely a collection of very old stories. People need to know what the church means by the story that it tells. This requires us to tell people about the church's teachings. However, we cannot simply outline the doctrine of the Trinity and assume that people will suddenly know what it means. Instead, we need to talk about how and why it arose. We need to explain what it meant when the church first said it and what it means today. We need our history.

Growth in understanding of our history, and the words that we use, is not automatic. That is why we go to school: we earn every piece of knowledge that we gain. This is true for individuals and for communities. Consequently, to be a thoughtful Christian requires serious study. Moreover, insights can be forgotten. Contemporary Christian thinkers often look to the past to find wisdom that has been lost.

Without tradition, which is really a fancy way of saying "memory," we lose all of the wisdom of past thinkers, who are often more sophisticated than we expect. In addition, we cannot make sense of what we say in the present, because all of our words are filled with the meanings given to them in past conversations. Tradition is indispensable, even in a world obsessed with progress.

Why do Christian positions on moral issues change?

The church is attentive to its history. That is why we began with some questions about the Bible, intelligence and tradition. However, we do not live in the past, even though we sometimes try very hard to do so. Life in the world is a process of growth and growth always implies change. This is most obvious in our actions; we do things which are different from what our ancestors did. Some people expect that Christian attentiveness to an unchanging God and a carefully built tradition will mean that our understanding of how humans behave should be permanent and unchanging.

As a matter of fact, however, Christian positions on moral issues do change. Our attitudes to such important aspects of human life as money, the environment and sexuality have shifted quite dramatically through the church's history. The world changes and our understanding changes. Christianity has always insisted that one should follow the best possible course of action in the circumstances which one faces. As circumstances shift and knowledge increases, we identify different courses of action as the best ones. We remain true to the principle that we ought to do good, but "good" takes on a different appearance.

Circumstances change, according to place and time. For academic reasons, my wife and I spent some time in Boston, having moved there from Ottawa. Driving habits in Boston are not the same as those in Ottawa. In Ottawa, people more-or-less follow written rules of the road. In Boston, when I requested a Driver's Handbook from the Department of Motor Vehicles, the clerk gave me a strange look and remarked that he didn't have many and wasn't sure what use I would have for one. Very rapidly, we discovered that driving in Boston is a continual process of aggressive negotiation, a form of duel at which the locals are experts. Plus, for some reason, the streets all meet at funny angles and rarely have signs. We adjusted; this was especially true for my wife, who had not done much of the driving previously. Unfortunately, when we returned to Ottawa, we took our Boston skills with us. We risked arrest for driving to the public endangerment for the next six months.

A change in place caused a change in actions. Moreover, the meaning of our actions changed. What was normal, or even timid, in Boston, was unacceptably aggressive in Ottawa. In Boston, we looked like nice, gentle people behind the wheel. In Ottawa, we appeared to be in need of a thorough attitude readjustment. Our actions meant something different; the best possible course of action changed.

This kind of change occurs all the time; we barely notice it. Similar changes occur over time; Boston originally had no cars, then it had a few and now it has an overabundance. Christianity faced a dramatic change of a practical kind in its earliest days. The first "Christians" were simply Jews who followed Jesus. They held to all of the Jewish laws, including those about diet. This was the right thing to do, for it showed their faithfulness to God. However, non-Jews soon started to take up the good news of Jesus. In their world, the Jewish laws did not carry the same implications about trust in God. The church, deciding that there is nothing intrinsically unclean about anything which God has made, announced that non-Jewish followers of Jesus did not need to maintain the Jewish standards of purity. The reasons for making choices about food shifted.

Similar shifts have happened since. Until the 16th century, the church vigorously forbade the lending of money at interest, because money was deemed to be infertile. It could not grow in the hands of the borrower, so the lender should not expect growth in the sum returned. Capitalism demonstrated that money could make possible a kind of fertility. Societies experienced growth and change as economies based on currency created a sort of flexibility impossible in cultures where barter is the norm. The church recognized that the justification for the rule no longer applied and changed its understanding of what constitutes misuse of money.[2]

Morality is always about an interplay of rules and judgements. We make judgements about what is good. The resulting actions become customary; people commonly do them, even if no law requires it. Some judgements become codified as laws. Our judgements and the actions which they require serve as rules for our society. Sometimes, these rules are written down as laws; on other occasions, such rules function as generally-held customs. Either as written laws or unwritten customs, they hold as long as they are generally understood to reflect the best courses of action for us.

2. Charles Hefling, "By Their Fruits," in *Our Selves, Our Souls & Bodies*, edited by Charles Hefling (Cambridge, MA: Cowley Publications, 1996), 159–161.

When the grounds for the rules no longer seem to hold, then the rules are changed. This is just as true for the church as it is for non-Christian society.

Practices often change simply because what the old practice means is no longer what it says, as in the case of lending money at interest. Rules may change for another reason, also. Sometimes our meanings change and we want to say something different. We will discuss that situation in the section entitled "Why does Christian thinking change?" First, though, we need to discuss what a "doctrine" is, so that we can be clear about the nature of beliefs.

What is a doctrine?

Derived from the Latin *docta*, the word "doctrine" simply means "things taught." I suppose that in its loosest sense, it might refer to anything that someone teaches someone else. However, we tend to limit the word to those things which have attained some degree of support in a field of study and, therefore, may reasonably be passed on to people who wish to understand that field. Every discipline, from cooking to astrophysics, has doctrines. A meat-cooking guide is just as much a collection of doctrines as any church statement, because such a guide teaches the aspiring cook what ought to be done in order to produce the desired result. A meat-cooking guide represents the accumulated wisdom of some part, at least, of the world of cooking experts and relays it to students of the art.

This is clear and straightforward, as far as it goes. However, most people do not learn to cook either solely by reference to books or by going to cooking school. Much of what we learn in this field (as in all fields) is gathered by listening to and observing others as they demonstrate to us how they cook. As we grow up, we watch members of our families cook and we internalize some of the approaches which they take, while rejecting others. When cooking becomes a routine part of our lives, we swap stories, advice, and recipes with acquaintances. In other words, what gets passed on as the doctrines of cooking is really a rather amorphous mass of information derived from a variety of sources. And some of that advice would make a master chef blanch (so to speak!).

That is one reason why cooking schools and cookbooks exist: they serve a kind of regulatory function. People who have studied and practised the art of cooking for years develop a deep understanding of the principles involved; they come to know something about what is helpful and what is unhelpful, what is right and what is wrong in the kitchen. By teaching what they have learned, they can undermine foolish advice which gets passed around and replace it with more accurate wisdom. Of course, schools of cookery are also centres of innovation; there people attempt new things, with the result that the art of cooking grows and changes. This is a good thing, too, since cooking styles of two hundred years ago would hardly suit present needs, diets or ingredients.

The church has its own ways of identifying doctrines: teachings about which there is some consensus and which are passed on to those who wish to understand Christianity (and perhaps even make some sort of commitment to it). In the church of the first eight centuries, councils (usually at the command of an emperor) met and made decisions for the whole body. We think of this as the time of the "undivided church" because the major divisions between the Eastern Church and the Western Church, followed by fractures within these bodies, had not yet occurred. The church was, however, riven by great struggles over matters of belief, sometimes causing riots in the streets and severe punishments at the hands of state officials. In the process, though, church leaders hammered out statements about central matters of Christian belief. The Nicene Creed, which many Christians recite during worship, came out of two 4th-century councils (one at Nicaea in 325 and one at Constantinople in 381). The Creed of the Council of Chalcedon (in 451) is not recited, but it established parameters for the church's beliefs about Jesus the Christ which continue to direct the vast majority of Christians today.

However, as we have seen, Christian theology did not stop after the last early church council (at Nicaea in 787). The Western Church adopted the practice of holding councils to make doctrinal decisions, although the councils were called by popes rather than emperors and the relationship between popes and councils was not always clearly defined. The Roman Catholic Church has continued the practice of holding councils called by popes. The Eastern churches have tended to emphasize the authority of early church councils, while governing with bishops and synods. Anglican churches make doctrinal decisions through bishops and synods, while Protestant churches use bishops, variously-named leaders, synods, conventions and other means to establish church teachings. All of these systems result in various sorts of statements which are doctrines.

This proliferation of systems for drafting doctrinal statements results in bewildering quantities of material. Often when we talk about Christianity as if we know what it is all about, what we really know is our own branch of Christianity. Other people might say quite different things.

Consequently, we have schools of theology and theologians who work in them, rather like the schools of cookery and the cooking experts who work in them. Theologians help Christians to sort through the reflections of councils, synods, theologians and other theological authorities from the whole of nearly two thousand years of explicitly Christian thought. In that sense, this book is a work of theology and you, by reading it, are taking a step toward becoming a trained theologian.

Theologians, like most academics, love to put things in categories. That helps them to work through issues in an orderly way. The various masses of doctrinal statements that we spoke about earlier demand some kind of categorization. We tend to distinguish among levels of authority ascribed to particular doctrines, as a means of clarifying the place of various beliefs in the whole of Christian teaching.

One way of doing this is by talking about a "hierarchy of truths," in which some beliefs are at the top and, therefore, are more important, while some are further down and less important. Roman Catholic theologians tend to use this notion, in part because it insists that all the parts are necessary; one must believe all of it, except that some parts are more obviously significant than others. This is called the "seamless web" understanding of the structure of systematic theology. Anglicans and some Protestants tend to speak about "core doctrines," that all Christians must hold, and "things indifferent" (commonly called *adiaphora* – a Greek term), which refers to important matters that may, nonetheless, be disagreed upon by Christians. The languages of "mere Christianity" or "simple gospel" tend to be popular among various Protestant groups, to designate what must be held by everyone. Sometimes they will talk about their own "distinctives" to identify their own particular contribution to the Christian world.

However one describes the relationship, some doctrines are universally held to be at the top or centre of Christian belief. Established in the earliest centuries of Christian history, these focus upon the salvation which God offers to the world. Christians believe that God is Trinity, three persons in one God. They believe that Christ is fully divine, one of the three persons of the Trinity, and took on full humanity in the person of Jesus of Nazareth. It is commonly held that one who does not accept these beliefs is not a Christian.

Associated with these doctrines is a commitment to two rites or sacraments (ceremonies). The first of these is baptism, which is the initiation rite for Christians. The other is the eucharist (also called "Holy Communion," " Sacrament of the Table," "Lord's Supper" or "Breaking of Bread"). Eucharist is celebrated regularly; Orthodox and other Eastern-rite, Roman Catholic, and Anglican churches ordinarily have it on a weekly basis. Other denominations vary; some hold it weekly, some monthly, and others quarterly. Very few Christians have such a celebration more rarely than that; only a tiny number (notably the Salvation Army) do not have it at all. For the vast majority of Christians, baptism and eucharist (discussed later in this book) are defining acts and have a central place in Christian belief and life.

One step lower on the ladder or further from the centre are doctrines which tend to define the specific emphases of particular groups. Lutherans, for instance, are well-known for their insistence upon belief in "justification by faith alone, through Christ alone;" this means that one enters into right relationship with God only by giving oneself to God in trust and that trust is itself a gift of God. Calvinists tend to emphasize the absolute greatness and might of God. Roman Catholics focus upon the centrality of the church to human salvation. Protestants who call themselves "Evangelical" (in the present context; this is a word with many uses) often preach the importance of personal conversion. These doctrines are part of what gives variety to Christianity, because they both identify and foster differences among Christian groups. Such doctrines may be accorded a slightly less important status than the teachings of the early councils; nonetheless, these teachings are often essential to the understanding of the gospel that gives identity to particular Christian groups. Consequently, they are usually held tenaciously. Like all other doctrines, these have arisen as answers to specific questions in particular historical circumstances. Without an understanding of that history, outsiders often have difficulty grasping why people regard these matters as so important.

In the process of trying to understand the gospel and apply it in their lives, Christian groups routinely establish doctrines by means of both formal and informal decision-making structures. Some of these amount to little more than passing fads and prove to be easily revisable; they are soon forgotten. An example might be the largely-informal, but very real, support given by liberal Protestants to the eugenics movement in the first half of the 20th century, which hinged upon a belief in human perfectibility and a commitment to caring for people by improving the gene pool. Today, that has largely disappeared from the collective religious memory; those who remember tend to be ashamed of the whole episode. By contrast, however, the Christian belief in the value of humanity and equality of persons before God – which ultimately issued in the anti-slavery movement led by William Wilberforce in England, the anti-oppression movement led by Martin Luther King, Jr. in the United States, and Desmond Tutu's part in the anti-apartheid movement in South Africa – has grown only more powerful and universal. These same movements have also required that some Christians, who supported slavery and oppression, amend their understanding of their own beliefs and change their way of life. The doctrine has become a general expectation of Christians and, moreover, of many societies. In an interesting way, teachings of this kind often cross denominational lines, just as the core doctrines do. The result is that Christians with very different denominational emphases can often work together on matters of common concern in their own historical contexts. Such Christians may even find themselves feeling more comfortable with people in other Christian (or even non-Christian) groups than with their own.

Something to remember about doctrines is that they are not altogether fixed in content. They are not like the batons in a relay race, which stay more-or-less the same while being passed from hand to hand. Instead, doctrines are passed from mind to mind, through the medium of language. One consequence of this is that doctrines are, and ought to be, rethought by every single person who holds them. They are unlikely to be held in precisely the same way by large groups of people, because each of us will interpret what we are taught in light of our own intellectual capacities and inclinations, as well as our own personal history. Moreover, our own personal stories are only pieces of a larger historical context, which has a tremendous impact on our understanding. Thus, doctrines develop as new questions arise and we develop new intellectual equipment to respond to those questions – which is why we discuss the issue of doctrinal development elsewhere.

Doctrinal development is one important reason for the existence of a variety of resources. We continue to need the Bible, because we must always be in conversation with the set of stories in which our identity as Christians is rooted. We need the larger Christian community, because growing and learning is never an individual process: conversation partners – in person, voice and print – are always necessary. We also need the specialized subset of the Christian community that is the scholarly theological community. Theologians help us to understand what has been said about doctrines in the past, while enabling us to weigh the significance, value and implications of present contributions. Theologians can also help people to understand some of the reasons for doctrinal change; these can be helpful to know when important questions arise and the Christian community begins to discuss a shift in long-held beliefs.

Why does Christian thinking change?

God does not change, but we do. One of the ways in which we change is in how we think. This has an impact on the sort of questions we ask and the kinds of answers we find.

Most traditional peoples, including Canada's First Nations peoples, communicate by telling stories. On parts of the West Coast of North America, totem poles were once an important aspect of community life. These poles told the stories of the families which erected them and linked those stories to the wider narrative of the world. They were stories made visible, in a culture where stories were the primary carriers of meaning.

The Bible is a collection of stories. It comes out of a Hebrew context, in which the central means of explaining the world and making decisions about life was through telling stories about God and God's relationship with the Hebrew people. However, even as the last parts of the Bible were being written, the world was changing. The Roman Empire was bringing the followers of Jesus into contact with Greek thought.

The Greeks told stories, too; their poetry and plays are some of the finest narratives of the ancient world. However, the Greeks also developed a philosophical tradition; in an activity which they called *theoria* (theory) they reflected upon the ideas which were presented in their stories, plays and public orations. Are these ideas consistent with one another? Do they appear to match the way in which the world works? Consequently, the Greeks asked and answered questions differently from other ancient peoples. Telling the stories was no longer enough; one had to explain the meanings and how they related to the meanings of other stories. The meeting between Hebrew narrative and Greek logic brought the birth of "theology" – a formal effort to reflect on the biblical stories.

The major Christian creeds are a product of this encounter with Greek thought; telling the stories of Jesus was insufficient, so the church had to identify which meanings of these stories were intended by the church and which were not. The biblical stories could be made to mean almost anything, but the church uses them because of what the church believes them to say. The creeds provide the church's explanation of those stories. That is why the church continues to recite them today.

Perhaps the most important shift which occurred with the appearance of the creeds is the introduction of language which is not from the Bible. In the creed often called "Nicene" (because it is derived from a creed drawn up at the Council of Nicaea in A.D. 325), God the Father and Jesus Christ are said to be "of one substance." This is a way of talking about the unity between the first and second persons of the Trinity. It means only that the Father is whatever the Son is and the Son is whatever the Father is, except that the Father is not the Son. This all gets a bit complicated, which is why this book includes other questions discussing the Trinity. The important thing to note right now is that the church could not simply continue to tell the stories of Jesus as they were originally told. There were too many questions about God and salvation left unanswered. The church needed to move into a different mode of thinking, which had its roots in the Greek discovery of logic. Christianity was changed forever by this shift and the ground was laid for a new way of thinking about religion.

In the Western world, in the Middle Ages, the church was the major source of understanding and moral direction. Christian thought had to grapple with a huge variety of questions. Moreover, there was a massive recovery of ancient learning, as scholars discovered and translated ancient writings. Great thinkers, such as Thomas Aquinas, used all of the available philosophical tools to construct systems of thought which integrated all knowledge of the world with Christian doctrines. This was the birth of "systematic" theology, with its effort to understand everything in relation to everything else; it is also the starting point of the university as we know it.

The key to understanding medieval thinking is to remember that medieval scholars valued inherited wisdom highly. One of the central purposes of Thomas Aquinas's great *Summa* was to demonstrate that any piece of wisdom received from the ancients – especially, but not only, Christian ancients – stood in firm agreement with any other such piece of wisdom, as well as correctly explaining the world as it is. The medievals believed that the world did not really change, in any essential way, so that knowledge gained in the past might be added to but could not be undermined or replaced.

In the 16th century, Martin Luther caused a great explosion. He pointed out that the church of his time did not look like the church of the Bible – things had changed in profound ways. Luther believed that the answer was to reconstruct the world of the biblical age. This approach was doomed from the start, because it began from the faulty assumption that the clock could be turned back. It cannot.

Instead, the modern world discovered history. Scholars began to realize that change happens. Indeed, in the 19th century, John Henry Newman demonstrated that even the most central of Christian beliefs had been formed over the course of time and would continue to develop. They could not simply be read from the Bible or the writings of ancient Christians. People ask new questions and answer them in new ways, so that the work of Christian thinkers is ongoing. Doctrines are not like a football, passed from hand to hand without any real change. Instead, they are passed from mind to mind, through the medium of language; both languages and habits of mind change. So do Christian beliefs.

The medievals were always in danger of being so committed to trusting the ancients that they did not notice changes occurring in their own time. We face the opposite hazard. Moderns can be so certain that new things are better than old that we fail to value our inheritance. We are formed by the habits and understandings which we receive. Our task is to judge how these things relate to the questions of our time. The present and future always come from the past.

The thought-world of our time is created, in large part, by the explosion of knowledge in the physical sciences. Our daily lives are formed by relationships with technology that comes out of scientific advance. I am composing this book on a computer, rather than scratching it on parchment. In order to think theologically today, we must have some sense of how our discipline of theology is affected by the physical sciences. That is the purpose of our next question.

How does theology relate to the physical sciences?

This is, of course, a huge question, with many possible answers. There are many discussion groups in which theologians meet with scholars in the physical sciences and many books in which eminent thinkers in both disciplines grapple with the complex issues involved. I will address only a small part of the question, but one which I think is important to many people. Can the physical sciences disprove theology? Can theology disprove the physical sciences? Can a world which has one also have the other? The last several hundred years have witnessed tremendous advances in scientific and technological thinking. For many people, the power of physics, biology, chemistry and other physical sciences is such that belief in God seems remote and pointless, making sense only as a psychological crutch for the weak. Are they being fair to theology?

As Bernard Lonergan has shown (*Insight: A Study of Human Understanding*, Toronto: University of Toronto, 1992), there is a very important basic similarity between theology and the physical sciences. Both rely upon a fundamental pattern of human activity which gives structure to any kind of investigation. Whenever we want to know something – whatever it is – we do four things: (1) gather information; (2) come to an understanding about the relationship, if any, among the various bits of data; (3) assess our conclusions, testing whether they are justified – in effect, judging the accuracy of our understanding; and (4) make decisions about the implications of the conclusions which we have reached – setting the stage for further actions. We always do these things, whether we are making soup or plotting the path of Halley's comet. This common pattern is one of the roots of our ability to share conclusions and debate all sorts of topics with each other. We can identify where our disagreements are. Do we disagree about the information which we have collected? Do we disagree in our understandings of the information or about the decisions which we have made as a consequence of our conclusions? In other words, our common way of thinking allows for discussion among very different people, in very different walks of life.

However, there is a basic difference between the physical sciences and theology which has an effect on the conversation. The physical sciences are governed by some rules which are helpful to them, but which do not apply to theology. The first of these rules is that only things which can, in principle, be measured are fit subjects for scientific study; in other words, modern physical sciences are strictly empirical. The second rule is that a conclusion may be regarded as true only if it can be verified by different people, again and again; in other words, every experiment must be repeatable.

These principles are of central importance to modern science and are the heart of its strength. The first rule identifies a very large, but carefully limited, field of study, while the second ensures that all assertions within that field can be checked, re-checked and built upon.

Reality, however, does not necessarily follow these rules. Some of the most important things in life cannot be measured, although we know that they are present; love, joy and peace are among these, as are anger, hatred and suffering. Our bodies provide physical indicators of these things, but the physical signs are not the whole. An elevated heartrate and the release of certain hormones may show that love of a sort is going forth, but surely love is more than a hormone-induced rush!

As for repeatability, we are well aware that some things occur only once. While it may be true that military errors get repeated, it is equally true that armies tend to fight in the same way as they did in the last war, since they have only previous experience from which to learn. This can be a problem for soldiers, because every war is different from the one before. Conditions change. The social sciences have come into existence to try to account for such variation; one of their tasks is to attempt predictions about human behaviour on the grounds of statistics drawn from history. However, their success rate is highly variable, precisely because things may happen only once in history.

Theology faces the awkward task of accounting for everything, whether that thing can be empirically measured and is repeatable or not. That means that theologians must work closely with people in other fields of study – and they do try, though the task is huge.

Whenever a theological conclusion depends upon evidence from the physical sciences, then the two must be in conversation; if the physical sciences revise their own conclusions (as routinely happens), then theologians must take that into account. Also, if theology misuses such evidence (as with attempts to dismiss evolutionary theories, such as Charles Darwin's), then scientists are right to contradict the theology.

However, some theological assertions draw much of their supporting evidence from conclusions which are not, in the strict scientific sense, measurable. Moreover some important parts of Christian and other theologies address occurrences which are not repeatable. No human experiment can generate another Jesus Christ, if Jesus is who Christians say he is. The fact of unrepeatability does not, in itself, render the Christian position indefensible. There is a whole range of matters which are – at least partly – beyond the range of criticism from the physical sciences; if theology is to be proved wrong on these things, then the proof must be on other grounds.

The physical sciences must also be clear about the limitations of the theories which they are continually expounding and testing. On occasion, scientists go beyond their own rules and make assertions which are essentially theological in nature. Stephen Hawking did this in *A Brief History of Time* when he suggested that scientists will "know the mind of God" when they have formed a complete theory which unifies all forces.[3] This is simply not the case; Hawking needs correction from theologians – and, perhaps, from fellow scientists – for exceeding the strict limits set by the rules of the physical sciences.

In other words, theology and the physical sciences each have legitimate ranges within which they work. The work of each area has an impact upon the other; the conversation must be ongoing. However, they cannot invalidate each other, because they do not always consider the same evidence; when they are examining the same evidence, they do not always do so in the same ways. Theology and the physical sciences are both necessary, while being distinct.

3. Stephen Hawking, *A Brief History of Time* (New York: Bantam, 1988), 175.

Can we know whether a religious claim is true or not?

If the methods of the physical sciences are not necessarily adequate to disprove theological assertions, then are we stuck? Must we accept that most of what religions have to say is beyond testing? Are all religious statements equally valuable and, therefore, equally valueless? Many people appear to think so. "The cafeteria of religions" seems to be open for people today; a common view is that one is best to take what works for oneself from the practices of any religion that one encounters. Many people believe that "Some things will help some people, while other things will help others. No religious activity has any particular connection to truth claims."

The problem with this attitude, of course, is that it can lead to any sort of insanity, from comparatively harmless good-luck charms through mass-slaughter of innocent people. Religion is not a tame thing that can be stored on any old shelf; it is an immensely powerful force which affects how each one of us understands the world. This means that we need to find a better way to discern truth from falsehood and good from evil than the simple criterion of what seems to serve my desire-of-the-moment.

Christian theology suggests that there are some basic criteria for a true religious viewpoint, criteria which are, I think, universally valid. You must be the judge, for these are decisions which must be made by every human being.

The story of the whole universe is one of creation and transformation, of being made and remade. Every person, place or thing comes into being as something, but with potential to be other things (as Aristotle rightly pointed out). Most people would agree that there are better ends and worse ends – since very few of us wish to die of starvation and dehydration in a barren desert. There is, indeed, something called good.

The only reason to bring anything into existence is love; this may be a love of the thing which is being created, or it may be a love of the purpose which that thing is called to serve, or it may be a combination of both. This implies that one of the characteristics of God (assuming that God exists) must be perfect love. God brings all things into being and helps them toward the end which God intends for them, if they wish to find it. A commitment to love and the consequent willingness to live creatively in the world are fundamental characteristics of true religion.

If this seems obvious to you, then I am pleased. You have made the judgement that the universe is a good and great gift and you are trying to respond to it in love. That is faith. There are people who do not think this way; they believe that evil is the primary characteristic of the world that they see. To these people, the world is an enemy to be enslaved or destroyed; it must serve their purposes or die. Hatred is in their hearts. Some of these people make religious claims; indeed, a startling number call themselves Christians. Any belief which has its roots in hatred and the zeal to destroy is thereby made false, for even if the statement (as a form of words) is technically correct, it remains truth twisted to serve false ends. What the person intends by those words is not true. It is a fundamental betrayal of God, the loving creator and redeemer.

In other words, there is a basic life-commitment which gives a foundation to a religious truth claim, or, indeed, to any truth claim.[4] It is: "Be in love." Mathematicians who have no love for numbers or the principles of mathematics are compromised from the start. Auto mechanics who have no love for engines are in similar trouble. A theologian, of any stripe, who has not been grasped by God's love will find the truth elusive, no matter how orthodox the logic. Here is the first test of any viewpoint which you hear: "Is the person presenting it apparently in love with God or only with that person's self-interest, or, even worse, with a call for the destruction of someone else?"

Similarly, there are some methodological commitments which, taken together, give us a basic method for analyzing a viewpoint (religious or other). The first is that we must pay careful attention to all of the available data. If there is evidence apparently going unconsidered, then we need to bring it into the conversation. In other words, we must be attentive. However, the greatest problem

---

4. Much of this account depends upon the work of Bernard Lonergan. See: Bernard Lonergan, *Method in Theology* (Toronto: Lonergan Research Institute, 1990).

with data is rarely a lack of it. Today, we are overwhelmed with information. Our difficulty is to know what to do with it. We need to find out what it means and how it is important. To do that, we must employ our best intellectual resources; we must be intelligent. Once we have come to an understanding of the available information, we cannot stop learning and revising, for none of us holds the final answer to every question. We must be open, prepared to listen to the conclusions which others have reached, while continually re-examining our own positions. In short, we must be reasonable. Finally, we must remember that understanding leads to action. We must strive to make our actions reflect our conclusions. We must seek to be responsible with our lives. All of this must always be driven by love.

The aforesaid guidelines provide us each with a way to undertake our own quests. If we follow the imperatives, "be attentive," "be intelligent," "be reasonable," "be responsible," and "be in love," then we can be confident that we will find the best answers available to us, at our respective levels of intellectual ability and in our different places and times. Moreover, we can ask whether those who are teaching us are also committed to following a path which reflects these values. We need always to consider the evidence which people give us in light of the limitations with which they live.

This is not, obviously, a simple solution to the problem of finding correct answers to religious questions. Conclusions are likely to be complex, partial and revisable. That is the nature of human understanding, in all areas. Have you ever tried to construct a diet according to the findings of health care researchers and professionals? Even the very best of studies finds only probabilities, with limited applicability. The advice about whether you should eat margarine or butter and drink white wine or red – or whether you should abstain from all fats except (perhaps!) fresh, cold-pressed, extra-virgin, olive oil while staying away from alcoholic beverages altogether – varies from authority to authority and from day to day. Even about the human body, which is so immediate to us and the subject of so much expensive study, we know far too little. Theology might be the most complex of the sciences, for it needs to find a relationship with all other sciences. There is no specialty which does not reflect upon the nature of God and God's creation. Therefore, we cannot expect that our answers will be complete and final; we can know something of what God communicates to us, but none of us fully knows the mind of God. Perhaps the most important imperative for our journey is one that has not yet been mentioned, though it is implied by everything that we have addressed: "Be humble."

At this point, some readers are likely staring at the page in complete bafflement. All of this stuff about investigation and imperatives is fine, as far as it goes, but what does it have to do with the authority of the Bible or the church or whatever has provided the grounding for religious faith in the average life? We need to bring together a few things that we have learned in our investigations. The first thing to remember is the priority of community; we learn things in groups, so that religious judgements are always affected by group judgements. This is where the church comes in; it tries to help us to live in love and humility, so that we can make good judgements. The church also provides data for religious decisions; the stories of the Bible and the history of Christian reflection about God's work in the world give us information upon which religious judgements may be based. This is evidence to which we must be attentive and which we must try to understand reasonably. Christian theology has something more to say about religious judgements, something that we will encounter in the next section; we have explicitly discussed the activity of the Holy Spirit in helping our discernment. At this point, I will say only that everytime we talk about love, we are identifying the work of the Holy Spirit.

What sort of language do we use to talk about God?

Before we move on to discussing specifically Christian theology, we need to say something about the nature of theological language. In theology, as in any other field of study, we work with analogies.

An analogy is a comparison, ordinarily between two entities – a familiar one and an unfamiliar one. An analogy helps us to understand something which is foreign to us, by identifying similarities and differences between it and something which we know a good deal about. We might, for example, need to explain what an ocean is, perhaps to a young child who has not experienced any body of water larger than a fairly ordinary lake. We could tell the child that an ocean is a body of water, just like that lake, but many times bigger. Boats go on both of them, except that the boats on an ocean can be huge ships. People swim in both of them, but swimming across the lake can be done by many reasonably-competent swimmers, whereas swimming across the ocean is an incredible task and rarely done. Also, the water in an ocean is full of salt. We have reasoned from a familiar entity to an unfamiliar one. The child will have learned something about an ocean and can even have something of a sense-based relationship with one, while having been nowhere near it.

In the process of constructing our analogy, we did two major things: we identified similarities between the two entities and we identified differences. The key to understanding analogical reasoning is to remember that it goes only so far and no farther. It can be helpful in illuminating similarities and, therefore, moving understanding forward. However, any two objects compared analogically will also have differences; those differences establish limitations on the usefulness of the analogy.

A common error in Christian theology is to take the name "Father" which we apply to the first person of the Trinity and drive the analogy implied by the term (from a human father to the first person of the Trinity) far beyond the meaning which it is intended to carry. We will talk at length elsewhere about the reasons for the name. Right now, though, we can say that it is not intended to carry any implication of sexual identity. The first person of the Trinity is not understood by theologians as having sex at all; that person has no body, let alone male genitalia, facial hair, Adam's apple or any other physical sexual characteristic. Yet, some people hear the term "Father" and automatically assume maleness. They insist that there is something intrinsically male about God – and then, of course, go on to justify all sorts of hierarchical practices on the basis of a terrible theological error. To insist that "Father" implies maleness in this case is a fundamental misuse of the analogy. The analogy has been pushed further than it goes; crucial differences between a human father and the divine Father are being treated as similarities, rather than being understood as the differences which limit the usefulness of the analogy.

Why do we use analogical language at all, then? Why not simply abstain from such awkward constructions? One reason is that all language is analogical, to some degree. All language depends upon a comparison between one thing and another, and one class of things with another class of things. That is precisely what is specified in a dictionary – the relationship between the term which you wish to understand, on the one hand, and various terms that you may already understand, on the other. You may, therefore, look up "horse," if you do not know what a horse is. You will then find out some of its characteristics: it is an animal, having four long legs, with a notable capacity for running, and so forth. The result ought to be that you will be able to construct something of a mental picture of a horse, based upon its relationship to other four-legged animals with which you are familiar.

The intellectual activity which you needed to undertake in order to do this is really quite important. That is because it points to the truly fundamental reason why we use analogy and why it is at the root of all language: we think analogically. All of our growth in understanding consists of this movement from the known to the unknown, through the construction of mental pictures. We use language to help ourselves establish relationships among different things, trying to recognize patterns which are understandable.

Theology works by analogy because all human reasoning proceeds that way. The analogies by which theology proceeds have an added level of complexity, though, when compared with veterinary analogies. A horse is a creature of time and space; it may be examined with the human senses, aided and magnified by various instruments. God is not a creature of time and space; moreover, the categories of theology – faith, hope, love, joy, and so on – may be temporal (meaning that time is relevant to them), but not spatial (they take up no space). God is not less real for being different from us, just as love is not less real for being different from horses, but the result is that our work with analogies will be more complex and fraught with danger than analogical work in veterinary medicine. Theology is a subtle science and calls for great care.

God

2

Who is the Christian God?

One common way to begin answering this question is to focus upon the things that God does for us, which we often name as creation, redemption and sanctification. These are technical terms, which I try to explain more thoroughly elsewhere in this book. We need to discuss them a bit here, however, because they are linked to the basic Christian name for God: Father, Son and Holy Spirit. We shall see that the link is not straightforward, though; we cannot simply take three tasks and link each of them to one divine person, as some people try to do. The doctrine of the Trinity is more complicated (and exciting) than that.

Creation, redemption and sanctification may be understood as one process: God bringing all things into being and forming them into suitable partners for God. Our ultimate purpose is to be with God and enjoy God; indeed, we are given the opportunity to join in God's life and work – that is the meaning of "eternal life." "Creation" is God's work of making all things, including us; "redemption" is God's work of turning all things, including us, toward God; "sanctification" is God's work of forming all things, including us, into God's likeness (in the sense of imbuing those things with divine qualities).

As we have seen before ("Can we know whether a religious claim is true or not?"), the only reason for making things is love. When we make things, love may appear in various forms. Sometimes we make things primarily because we need them or the money which they will bring; we may love the products of our labours, but there is some element of self-interest in our work. So long as self-interest does not dominate the process and compromise the product, love toward the other remains. When self-interest takes over and the product loses its integrity, then evil has found its home.

This does not happen to God, because God does not want or need anything, in the sense of being inadequate without it. This is part of the point about God being the Creator. If God had needs, then God would be dependent upon something or someone else for God's existence. That other being must exist before God does, or else God would not have what God needs in order to be God. Either that other being would be the ultimate Creator, or there would be no ultimate Creator and existence would merely consist of an endless chain of prior beings, each one implying one before.

So God has no reason to act out of self-interest. God acts only for the good of the creatures which God creates. God is free from all evil. God creates all things out of pure love, manifested in giving to creation the joy of being. God speaks creation into life; in doing so, God gives the opportunity to participate in God's life.

This means that God does not merely bring us into being; God also seeks to help us grow into the best "us" that we can become. That is the meaning of the language of "redemption" and "sanctification." We often trap ourselves in our misdeeds. We become so focused upon our own short-term self-interest that we lose sight of what is best for others, or even ourselves. In the process, we fail to see that our good can only be found in a right relationship with God. We forget that we cannot fulfil the purpose of our lives if we do not stay in unity with the Creator who gives us that purpose. God establishes this relationship with us through Jesus Christ. As creation happens through the Word, so does redemption.

The Holy Spirit is the animating principle of the world, the breath that God breathes into all creation, in order to give life to it. The Holy Spirit, therefore, is an agent of creation and also of the Incarnation, which is the birth of Jesus (more about this in further chapters). The Holy Spirit also plays a central role in sanctification, which is helping the whole of creation to live God's life rather than seeking death. Following our own short-term self-interest is not really in our interest; it leads to destruction. Life and meaning are found in fulfilling the purposes given to us by the Creator. Sanctification is the ongoing process of transforming creation into the true self which God wants for it. This means giving real life to the creation – which is, you may have noticed, rather similar to the definition which we gave for "creation." Sanctification is the process of giving creation the opportunity to be what it ought to be and is, therefore, an extension of the process of creating.

The Christian God is understood as the one who brings us into being, into relationship and into fulfilment. The point of every aspect of Christian life is to thank God by taking those blessings to ourselves, enjoying them and giving thanks to God for providing them.

Why does the Bible show God doing things which appear to be evil?

This is one of the most difficult questions which Christians face. It has two answers of which I am aware (I suspect that other people will have other answers). The first response has to do with the nature of God, while the second is rooted in the relationship between humans and the biblical text.

If God is, indeed, the great Creator, Redeemer and Sanctifier of whom we have spoken, then God is very likely to do things which we cannot understand. As Gandalf, a wizard in J. R. R. Tolkien's *The Lord of the Rings*, comments: "Even the very wise cannot see all ends." The wisest and most knowledgeable of humans does not know the reasons for all things that occur, nor the purposes which all things serve.

Indeed, we have a difficult time identifying the implications and consequences of our own actions. There is great uncertainty around every decision which we make and everything that we do. We make chance remarks in conversation, with the best of intentions, and discover later that we have done great harm. We give cheery greetings to people and find out that, all unawares, we have transformed their lives. What is true on the simplest level is also true on the most complex. Sciences, today, proceed statistically. They discuss probabilities, rather than certainties. We have immense debates about global warming, drug therapies and genetically-modified food products, for example, precisely because the best that we can do is to generate models which account for as much data as possible and suggest scenarios for the future, with some indication of their likelihood.

Of course, when we discuss human actions, there are issues of human limitations and sinfulness attached. By contrast, knowing the loving God enables us to trust, even if we cannot always see, that God is bringing about the best, somehow. God is always bringing about God's reign, though sometimes we cannot see it. This is the great puzzle of God's loving justice: God does what is just (which is whatever brings God's kingdom), whether or not we can identify it. God has power that is not our power. God helps us to do God's will, but God's accomplishments do not rest on our actions. In a metaphorical sense, God has hands which are not our hands.

This is the answer that God gives to Job, in the Bible. The Book of Job is an interesting piece; it has a carefully constructed, literary, style. Some scholars think that it was composed as a play. Its topic is the age-old question: "Why do bad things happen to good people?" Job is a faithful servant of God, but he undergoes a series of disasters. Along the way, he argues with his wife and friends about the meaning of his suffering and the appropriate reaction to it. Job composes a case against God, arguing that the righteous are mistreated, while evildoers thrive. God comes to answer the case.

> Then the LORD answered Job out of the whirlwind:
> "Who is this that darkens counsel by words without knowledge? . . .
> Where were you when I laid the foundation of the earth? Tell me, if you have understanding.
> Who determined its measurements – surely you know!" (Job 38:1–5a)

Indeed, God goes on at great length, emphasizing the might with which God works and the unknowable complexity of God's activity. In a way, this is one of the all-time greatest non-answers in the history of literature. A statement that the whole issue is too complicated for Job to understand does not really resolve the problem. In another way, though, it is the only answer possible. If I can barely comprehend the implications of passing conversations in my daily life, then how could I expect to understand the meanings of everything that happens in the created order and the ways in which all things affect all other things? We strive to know what we can; that is a good thing. However, to think that we know all things is merely *hubris*, the arrogant pride which claims that we are God. That is a pride which never goes unpunished, because our actions always have unintended and unexpected consequences: these will affect us in surprising (often unpleasant) ways if we are not willing to admit the limitations of our knowledge and, therefore, live in the awareness that we neither completely understand nor fully control the world.

There is another, even more complex, reason for the questionable actions and dubious motives which are sometimes attributed to God, either in the Bible or elsewhere. The biblical text was composed by people who were trying to understand God and the world. The church has always insisted that they did so with divine leading, with the power of God flowing in and through them. This is what the doctrine of "inspiration" means: that God breathed God's life – the movement of the Holy Spirit – into the authors. That, however, is some distance from the assertion that the authors were incapable of error and possessed of the final answer to every relevant question. They passed down to us what they knew, however they discovered it.

Perhaps the most helpful example of what I am trying to suggest comes from the Gospel of Luke. The author clarifies the source and purpose of the book right at the very beginning:

> Since many have undertaken to set down an orderly account of the events that have been fulfilled among us, just as they were handed on to us by those who from the beginning were eyewitnesses and servants of the word, I too decided, after investigating everything carefully from the very first, to write an orderly account for you, most excellent Theophilus, so that you may know the truth concerning the things about which you have been instructed. (Luke 1:1–4)

The author has undertaken careful research and seeks to hand on the truth as completely and faithfully as possible. This does not guarantee absolute freedom from error. It does, however, suggest to us that the Gospel of Luke is as fair a representation of the early church's understanding of Jesus (at least, that part of the early church with which the author is familiar) as the author could make it. On the other hand, even that assertion is still conditioned by a recognition that we each have our own way of understanding things, and this has an impact on whatever we say or write. That is one reason for the differences among the four Gospels: they attest to the same events, but present them in distinct ways.

Ultimately, then, we can look at the story of Noah and the flood without making the assumption that it is a narrative about out-of-control divine rage, which leaves God feeling repentant when the anger wears off. Instead, we can begin by recognizing that this particular story is in the language of myth; it describes in cosmic terms a fear of disorder and destruction with which humanity always lives (as we see in the discussion about global warming, today). Nobody ever assembled two of every kind of creature (Genesis 6:19–20) or two of every unclean creature and 14 of every clean creature (Genesis 7:2–3) on a boat. Moreover, the rainbow is neither more nor less a sign of God's maintenance of the world than any other aspect of creation. All of this is simply to say that the story is not historical, in the modern sense.

On the other hand, we can look around us and see evidence of the evil that humanity perpetrates. If we take careful stock of it, we can understand how monumentally-destructive shifts of nature might be understood as divine retribution. Evil has natural consequences. The story, therefore, stands as a warning against doing evil to others and the created order. At the same time, the world continues to exist and show forth God's love; the world is still beautiful, demonstrating that God is in charge and has not forgotten the created order.

The narrative remains, however, one human interpretation of a natural convulsion. We cannot easily say how God is working in relation to any particular event, whether of specifically human origin or simply a part of the workings of our universe (or some admixture of both). That is why we believe in God. Our ultimate trust is not in a book or in people, but in the God who loves us and cares for us.

How did the Christian understanding of God develop?

The Christian understanding of God did not appear all at once. It is not altogether to be found in the biblical stories, though they provide much of the data with which theologians work. No one thinker in the late-biblical or early post-biblical period simply elaborated all of these things for the church. Instead, the church needed to meditate on many questions and considerations before arriving at some common assertions which could be stated on behalf of the whole church.

The documents included in the Bible set the stage for the conversation. In the Hebrew Scriptures, we meet a God who creates all things. God also cares for people and creatures and tries to reconcile them to Godself. We see, especially, a people who understand themselves as belonging to God in a covenantal relationship. A covenant is a sort of agreement, often with a legal or quasi-legal status, identifying mutual commitments that people have with each other. It is rather like a contract, except that contracts tend to be impersonal, while covenants often focus upon a deeply-felt sense of shared responsibility. At the heart of the Hebrew people's relationship to the Lord is the divine statement: "You shall be my people, and I will be your God" (Ezekiel 36:28, though the same point is made in many places). This defined all of their social and political ordering, family relationships, relationships with the land, economic activities and military activities, as well as their formal worship rituals.

In the Hebrews, we also encounter a people with a strong sense of hope in God, a belief that God is acting in the world and will bring the world completely into God's order. That is what is meant by the "kingdom of God": any situation in which God's work is evident is a manifestation of the kingdom (God reigns there) and the ultimate moment of the kingdom is anticipated as the time when all of creation will do God's will.

In the New Testament, we find that the Creator God becomes human in order to give to creation its true meaning, bringing fulfilment to the kingdom. We also discover that the breath of

God, which gives life to all things, lives in us and enables us to become what God has given us the power to be. However, the church took some time to agree that this was its understanding and clarify what this means, because the stories can be read in a variety of ways.

The first question which demanded attention was this: Is Jesus the Christ actually God, or merely a representative of God, with the same creaturely origins as other created beings? At first, different followers of Jesus said different things. Because of its origins as a Jewish sect, Christianity contained a significant number of people who could not accept Jesus as anything more than a prophet of God. Others, influenced by Gnosticism (a belief system with Zoroastrian roots, which insisted that all material stuff is evil and all spiritual stuff is good), argued that Christ could not be human; they insisted that God had merely adopted the body of a person and dropped it when it was convenient.

Ultimately, though, the question was forced by a man named Arius, who was a leading Christian in Alexandria. Founded by the Greeks in Egypt, Alexandria was a major centre of thought and culture in the days of the Roman Empire. Arius could do two things which made him a decisive figure in the controversy: (1) with rigorous training in Greek philosophy, he could do logic; and (2) he could read the Bible. Arius accepted the monotheistic principle, which asserts that God must be indivisible; if there is more than one god, then ultimate being and power is shared. If it is shared, then it is not complete or ultimate. After all, what would happen if the two gods disagree? Either one must defeat the other and prove to be the more powerful or the *cosmos* is at a standoff, with two equal powers at odds with one another. Moreover, in Arius's reading of the Bible, Jesus the Christ seems to be inferior to the Father, though greater than all other creatures. Arius, therefore, argued that Jesus is a creature, made by the Father to show forth divine glory to creation. "There was a time when he was not;" Jesus is not eternal. He is divine, in that he reflects God's character to creation and is above all of the rest of the created order. However, he is not God.

In response to this theology, Christians discovered that they were doing two things which were decisive for the life of the church. First, they worshipped Jesus as God; indeed, they baptized people in the three-fold name of Father, Son and Holy Spirit. If that was the focus of their worship and at the centre of their entry rite, then they were making an assertion about unity between God the Father and Jesus, the Son. They were saying that Jesus is something more than a representative of the Father, no matter how faithful. Second, they preached that God, in Jesus the Christ, had transformed all of creation and unified it all with Godself. We will discuss the meaning of this in the section on salvation and the question about the Christian gospel. For the moment, we need to understand the decisive consideration of early soteriology (theology about salvation, from the Greek *sotero*) which went like this: "that which He has not assumed He has not healed; but that which is united to His Godhead is also saved."[1] This means that the salvation of all of creation depends upon God – true God – becoming united with all aspects of the created order. If Jesus is not truly God, then salvation has not happened and is not happening to us or anyone/anything else. A mere representative or message-bearer could only have told us about God and God's love, whereas the Son became one of us and transformed us and the whole created order.

At the Council of Nicaea (325), then, the church decided that the Father and the Son are "of one substance." This does not imply that they are made of the same stuff, since God is not made of stuff. It means only that whatever the Father is, the Son is also. Both are truly eternal, having no birth and undergoing no change. Following the same reasoning, the church declared that the Holy Spirit is co-eternal with the Father and the Son (at Constantinople in 381). The three persons are one God.

These assertions raised further questions, of course, and some of them will be discussed in other places (notably the questions on the Father, Jesus the Christ, and the Holy Spirit). There are some important things to note here, though. Some people are inclined to treat the early church councils as simple matters of ecclesiastical and

---

1. Gregory of Nazianzus, *To Cledonius the Priest Against Apollinarius (Epistle CI)*, in *Nicene and Post-Nicene Fathers, Volume 7: Cyril of Jerusalem and Gregory Nazianzen*, edited by Philip Schaff and Henry Wace (Peabody, MA: Hendrickson, 1994), 440.

state politics. These things played a part – not always pretty – in driving forward the discussion. However, the process was one of asking and answering serious questions, engaging the best minds and methods available at the time. Moreover, these were not irrelevant exercises in philosophical hairsplitting. The church's conclusions were driven by the exigencies of the gospel and the church's worship life. These two issues are what bring the church into existence and maintain its life. Nothing could be more important to it, which is why the statements of these early councils continue to define the meaning of being Christian.

What do we mean when we speak of God as "eternal"?

More than once, we have used the word "eternal" to describe God. However, we have not clarified the meaning of this very important term. Since it is commonly used in a way that is unhelpful for our purposes, I will try to explain what contemporary theologians generally mean when they speak of God as eternal. The fundamental difficulty with the word "eternal" is that we can only define it negatively – by what it is not. This is because we are not eternal; in fact, the word "eternal" says something about characteristics which are intrinsic to being God and constitute a sort of antithesis to being human. "Eternal" means "not conditioned by time or space."

Time is a very complicated thing, in many ways. We who live in an intellectual world partly conditioned by the physics of relativity are aware that time can do funny things. However, prior to the complexities is a rather simple definition: time is the measurement of the succession of occurrences. Roughly, that means that time refers to happenings coming after other happenings. The complications appear because movement and distance affect the "before" and "after." A year in a craft travelling nearly at the speed of light occurs while more than one year is passing according to a clock in a building on Earth.

God

I am pleased to say that we can step aside from the problems of relativity, however, because the point of suggesting that God is eternal is that God is not affected by time at all. In God, there is no succession of occurrences; nothing happens before or after anything else. St. Augustine stated it beautifully: "God dwells in the simultaneity of eternity."[2] God is simultaneously present to all times. Also, God has no origin, so that there was not a time when God came into existence. God does not change, for that would imply a succession of occurrences in God; God would have been in one state and then moved into another. Being eternal means that God simply *is*.

If God is truly eternal, then God is also not conditioned by space. This means that God is present in and to all things, everywhere. There are no places from which God can be banished. As the Psalmist says:

> Where can I go from your spirit?
> Or where can I flee from your presence?
> If I ascend to heaven, you are there;
> if I make my bed in Sheol,[3] you are there.
> If I take the wings of the morning
> and settle at the farthest limits of the sea,
> even there your hand shall lead me,
> and your right hand shall hold me fast.
> If I say, 'Surely the darkness shall cover me,
> and the light around me become night',
> even the darkness is not dark to you;
> the night is as bright as the day,
> for darkness is as light to you. (Psalm 139:8–12)

The Bette Midler song which announces that "God is watching us from a distance" (Julie Gold, 1985) is not merely scary and depressing; it is also fundamentally erroneous. God cannot watch

---

2. Augustine of Hippo, *Confessions*, translated by Henry Chadwick (Oxford, Oxford University Press, 1992), XI, vii; 226.
3. Sheol is the place where the dead go and lead a shadowy existence. No notion of judgement or punishment is attached to Sheol. The Hebrew understanding is that everyone goes to Sheol after death.

us from a distance because God cannot be at a distance from us. God is present in every person and animal, every rock and tree, every skyscraper and car, every ... you name it: God is everywhere.

The "simultaneity of eternity" affects both time and space. God is present to all times and all places at once. This, of course, is not true of humans. Time and space are fundamental to our identity. We are born, we live, and we die. We have bodies that are involved in every aspect of our lives, conditioning every aspect of our existence.

Our temporal and spatial natures condition our thinking, so that whenever we wish to understand anything we must begin with creatures of time and space. That is part of why we use analogies, as we saw in our discussion of analogy ("What sort of language do we use to talk about God?"). That is also a fundamental part of the reason why the Bible provides many stories of God that seem to imply that God changes God's mind or moves from one emotional state to another. We live in stories. Stories are successions of events that are understood to have meaning. Our encounters with God and our moments of growth in understanding God are always part of our personal stories, which in turn are tiny parts of the larger story which is history. Consequently, when we tell the narrative of God's involvement in our lives and our larger world, we always speak of God in a way which makes God historical. God seems to move and change. If traditional Christian theology is correct and God is eternal, then that is simply a reflection of our limited understanding. God does not change.

This implies that everything which God does, God does in the one act of existing. This idea is rather mind-bending. It is one of the most difficult aspects of Christian theology for humans to think, which is probably why we tend to lose this insight from time-to-time and start to devise theologies around the idea that God changes, learns and grows. Such theologies place God in history with us and have God guessing at the future in the same way that we do. If God is eternal, then God simply is and is present to all times and places at once. This suggests that all moments are permanent moments for God. Change and growth are real, but they are the reality of created life. God is still, in the sense of being without movement. In that stillness, everything that has been and will be, always is.

Freedom is something which we will discuss in a later section. The argument that I will make there is that freedom is not merely being able to do whatever one wishes, changing one's mind as appetites and inclinations lead; instead, freedom consists in the ability to know and do the good. That is a very important argument, because it touches on the nature of God, as well as on the created order. God is absolutely free, in the sense of being able to know and do the good. That is all that God can do. On the other hand, God does not make choices; God possesses nothing of this kind of freedom. All that God is and does is simply given in God's person. What God is and does is all locked into place, unchanging, irreversible. Happenings that appear to us to be a consequence of God changing God's mind cannot be so. God is who God is.

I find this doctrine to be a comfort. God is intimately present in and to everything, knowing all of it in every detail. Because all that I am and all that everything else is are already known to God, God truly does know what is best for me. I cannot shock God or present God with surprises. More importantly, I cannot cause a situation which is beyond God's capacity to redeem, for everything is already in God's "hands." The eternality of God is, indeed, a blessing.

Why do we believe in the Trinity?

The Trinity is sometimes treated as if it were simply an obscure add-on to Christianity, stuck in by theologians to complicate life. Most Christians accept belief in the Trinity because such belief is rooted in the teachings of Jesus and the church. The Bible does not speak about the Trinity, but the text contains a solid body of evidence for the unity of Father, Son and Holy Spirit. However, even the most dedicated Christians tend to regard this as the church's most confusing doctrine, so they frequently ignore it. In fact, the assertion that God is Trinity is the most important thing that Christians have to say. Everything else flows from this.

Christians believe that God is a Trinity, three persons being one God. Think of the way that a story is written and you will begin to understand what we mean.[4] A story begins with a general idea, such as "I will write about penguins." The idea is like the one whom we call Father. In my head, I fill out the idea with details; the detailed story is the child, or son, of the original idea. Having worked out how the story will read, I respond to it and judge it to be good or to be in need of changes; this is the spirit responding to the composition. The idea, the composition and the response to it are all still the same story.

In the creation of the story, the idea always remains in the writer's head; nobody else ever sees the original idea. It has no body, just as the Father has no body and no sex. The Father is not male – "Mother" would be an equally helpful term, but we tend to stick with "Father" because Jesus used it and replacing it with similarly gender-laden language would seem to imply that sex was somehow the point in the first place. The idea is "father" to the story, because the script comes from it and is directed by it. The essence of the script is found in the idea.

The expression of the idea is the child, the "Son" of the idea. It proceeds out of the idea. This expression is the story, with all its details filled in. In a perfect situation, the script perfectly reflects the originating idea; the "Son" fully and precisely shows forth the "Father." This is true of God: the Son is the exact image of the Father.

Note that this is true even when the story does not get written down; it may exist, in complete form, in the head of the author. A story need not be embodied (which is what "incarnate" means) to convey the idea. Famous writers are known for carrying lengthy portions of their work in their heads, prior to writing, and great composers often do so with musical compositions. Similarly, the Son need not be incarnate in order to communicate the Father's identity.

However, the story may become visible and tangible. It may be written down, becoming a text. This, being a communication of the

---

4. This analogy is based upon the book analogy which Dorothy L. Sayers outlines in *The Mind of the Maker* (San Francisco: Harper SanFrancisco, 1987).

idea (the "Father"), is a child of the idea. It is a visible manifestation of the Son. In our analogy, we can speak of two cases in which God has undertaken such manifestations – conveying who God is.

One manifestation occurs as God brings into being the created order. This is a real, though partial, self-communication of the divine idea. Any act of creation will, inevitably, convey something of the nature of its author. God's perfection means that the created order is a perfect, though very partial, reflection of God's identity. The other example is the Incarnation of the Son of God, which is the birth of Jesus the Christ in the world. Jesus the Christ shows the Father more completely than the created order can, because in Jesus the Christ we see the Son in person. Creation merely reflects an aspect of God's personality. By contrast, the Son is God and is able to tell us and show us, in a very direct way, who the Father is and what the Father means by all this.

A story is never complete if it does not garner some response from somewhere. Indeed, no narrative can exist if an author does not respond to the promptings of the mind which cause that person to write. The author must attend to the idea and must respond to it with words, if a story is going to be written. Moreover, they must be the right words – true to the idea – if the story is to be a good one and the author is going to be satisfied with the results. In other words, the author must respond with love to the idea and must lovingly express it. In our analogy, the Holy Spirit is that loving response to the idea – God's answer to God's self-expression that is the Son.

If the story remains in the author's head and is never told or written down on paper, then the only response to it comes from the author's self. This is what God would be like, if God had not made the created order. However, in an interesting twist, God has made a creation that is able to respond to God. We can think, talk and act. That God wants a creation that can respond to God in love says something about who God is. God's interest in a potentially loving, rather than merely loved, creation is what we are talking about when we speak of God as being a "personal" God: God loves the creation and knows that creation must live in love if it is to fulfil its own nature. That is the most important way in which creation is made in the image of God.

There are differences, of course, because creation reflects an aspect of God's identity but it is not God. One very obvious difference is that doing the right thing is optional for humans; we may choose not to. The Spirit helps us to respond to God in good and right ways, enabling the response in love which is so necessary to life.

God has made a creation which is capable of responding to its Creator – a peculiar starting point. Reality gets stranger, though. A further twist is that God (the author) has chosen to write Godself into the story, as a participant in it. The Son becomes visible, to show and explain the meaning of the whole book (this is when the Son takes on sexual characteristics, which are not an aspect of the second person of the Trinity). The Incarnation of the Son helps us to understand the story, so that we can play our parts correctly, in the right Spirit.

There can be no story without an idea, a composition and a response to it. There cannot be a creation without these three things, either. That is part of the reason why Christians believe in the Trinity. We also believe that creation is more exciting and meaningful because God the Trinity creates us to share in it and both shows us how to enjoy it (through Jesus) and gives us the power to love it (through the Spirit).

There is more to our belief in the Trinity, though. We are also thankful that God has made a creation that can respond to God, work with God and show God's love.

In the story that I described God as writing, something unique happens. The writer jumps into the middle of the story. God takes on all the usual limitations that a movie character would, including all the joy and suffering. God explains the meaning of it all and completes the narrative by demonstrating the triumph of good over evil, of creativity over destruction.

We are, of course, discussing the story of human existence. Jesus the Christ is truly God; he took on all of what it means to be human. He even died a shameful and dishonourable death, showing that we dishonour God and the people who do what God asks. Jesus rose from death, returning to share life with his followers, showing that God's creativity is more powerful than death and destruction. Jesus explains the whole meaning of life to humanity and invites us to share life with him. He invites us, all humanity, into God's family.

We cannot live life, God's life, without God's help. The Holy Spirit (with the Father and the Son) is God present in all things. The Holy Spirit gives us the power to become like Jesus, living creatively and triumphing over destruction.

The one whom we call Father; the one whom we call Son, incarnate in Jesus the Christ; and the Holy Spirit are one God. The three persons are a *unity*. They know and will the same things, in absolute oneness, unlike humans, who differ in understanding and inclination. If they were not in such unity, then they would continually disagree, just as the gods of Greek and Roman stories do. Moreover, if Jesus were not God, one with the Father, then Jesus could not show us who the Father is. If the Holy Spirit were not God, then the Spirit could not help us to live God's life – the Spirit would lead us into some other kind of existence.

Jesus is God and shows us who God is. The Holy Spirit enables us to live God's life. Therefore, we believe in the Trinity.

Who is God the Father?

This is a tough one to answer, because "No one has ever seen the Father," as Jesus says in the Gospel of John (1:18). Nobody has seen the Father, but we have plenty of evidence of the existence of this, the first person of the Trinity. I have spoken already of the need for an original idea, if any creation is to occur ("Why do we believe in the Trinity?"). The one whom we call "Father" is similar to that idea, except we have reason to believe that the Father has personality, in the sense of being able to communicate in love. The awkward thing about the previous sentence is that God's self-communication is the Word, the Son, so that everything that we say about the Father must be said in light of the Son.

The Father, then, is the root and holder of all form and meaning. Everything that comes to be does so in accordance with the Father's design. The primary evidence of the Father's existence is simply that things come into being. Unless all of what we call "the created order" is merely a cosmic accident, there must be a Father (though you may prefer other names – as some people do).

God's communication to us tells us what the Father is like. Assuming the correctness of the Christian belief in the Trinity, then the Son is an exact representation of the Father. Indeed, the Son *is* the Father's self-understanding; the Son is the single expression of God's intellect. Therefore, what the Father is, the Son is also, except that the Father is not the Son and the Son is not the Father. This is a complicated way of saying that the Father tells only the truth, the whole truth and nothing but the truth – both to Godself and to us. How much of it we can understand is, of course, another issue.

The Father communicates Godself in two ways: (1) through creation; and (2) through the Incarnation. The created order does not merely assure us that God exists. It also tells us that God loves us and all of creation. This follows from what we have said previously about God's self-sufficiency. God does not need to create in order to be or in order to be God. However, God creates because God is love and the nature of love is to love both the lover and the other. In other words, if you truly love, then you will love yourself and other people, other things. God is love as we know love, only without the limits which always affect our capacity to love. God loves everything, without limits or compromises. God creates in order to give love. God creates because life is the greatest gift possible and God has the power to give it.

The whole thrust of the biblical story about God is that the Father does not merely bring things into being and then leave them alone, which is what some people (called Deists) have suggested. Instead, the Father wants the created order to enjoy living, which it can do only if it fulfils its intended purposes. The Father knows those purposes, because the Father knows Godself completely and all of creation completely. The Father possesses the ultimate purpose and design for all things and, therefore, understands what will lead to true happiness and fulfilment for all things.

The Father does not wish to keep this knowledge secret; it is communicated in the act of making and in the Incarnation, so that we might know the meaning of our lives and be able to participate in the divine life which is offered to us. The Father, therefore, participates in our transformation, our salvation, by speaking to us through the Son. Until we know something about the Son, however, all of this remains unhelpfully vague. This is, as it happens, a restatement of one of the reasons for Christian belief in the Trinity: a distant and uncommunicative Creator is of no help to the human condition, while a Creator who comes to us and lives with us as a human can transform our lives. Thus, we now turn to discussing the Son, the second person of the Trinity.

Who is Jesus Christ?

1. Introduction: Jesus and the Trinity

Christians tend to emphasize Jesus the Christ; the term "Christ" even appears in the label which we apply to ourselves. "Christ" means "anointed one;" it is a title, rather than a name, and it applies to royalty. Saying "Jesus Christ" is a lot like saying "King Jesus." Christians believe that Jesus rules over everything. The complication in the theological conversation, and one which accounts for a great many differences among Christians, is defining that kingship. What is it about Jesus that makes him king and what does his kingship look like? How does it help us to understand our own lives and world, as the Father desires?

Some Christians focus upon Jesus's death on a cross. They talk about Jesus's blood having a kind of cleansing power, which washes away sin. Often, these people call for an individual conversion, a radical change of life which reorients the self toward the heavenly afterlife. Other people emphasize Jesus's teaching about the kingdom and social justice. They call for a fundamental transformation in the human community and its relationship to the weakest and poorest. Sometimes these two views clash and those who hold one come to regard the others as enemies. This is an unfortunate result of a partial understanding of Jesus the Christ.

As far as I can tell, the best approach to understanding who Jesus is and what he does for us involves considering every aspect of his work on earth and in heaven, so far as we know about it. The Prologue to John's Gospel (John 1:1–18) gives the conversation about Jesus its starting place. "In the beginning was the Word, and the Word was with God, and the Word was God. He was in the beginning with God. All things came into being through him, and without him not one thing came into being" (John 1: 1–3a). This is a tremendously important assertion, for it is at the root of our Trinitarian theology.

When Christians read Genesis 1, they understand that the Triune God is creating. Bringing things into existence is not an activity solely undertaken by the Father, the first person of the Trinity. Instead, all three persons of the Trinity are involved. The Father participates by expressing the original conception of everything through the Father's Word: the Son. In the story, everything that God creates is spoken into existence. Of course, the Father has no mouth, so we are using the language of analogy (see: "What sort of language do we use to talk about God?"). However, the analogy is an important one. When we speak, we express ourselves. Even when we intend to mislead, we are, nonetheless, revealing something of what and who we are. God cannot be misleading without undermining Godself and the creation that God so lovingly makes; God's self-expression can only be accurately revealing about who God is. God's Word, the Son of God (whom we call Christ) can only be an altogether true and honest representation of Godself.

All creation is a communication of Godself, so it always occurs through the Son. The Father, being eternal, is never distant from the created order. The eternal is never at any distance from anywhere. However, the Father is also never perceptible to creation; the first person of the Trinity cannot be seen, heard or felt. All that we ever meet is God's self-communication – what God says about Godself – and that is what Christ is. As the Prologue to John says, "No one has ever seen God. It is God the only Son, who is close to the Father's heart, who has made him known" (John 1:1–18). "All things have been handed over to me by my Father, and no one knows the Son except the Father, and no one knows the Father except the Son and anyone to whom the Father chooses to reveal him" (Matthew 11:27).

John 1 tells us something else about the Son, which is that he is the universal Word. He is "the light of all people" (John 1:4). The Greek for "word" is *logos*. *Logos* refers to many things besides what we call words. It refers to the mind and its products. Note that *logos* is part of the root of many names of scientific disciplines: theo*logy*, bio*logy*, geo*logy*, etc. That is because these are areas in which we make a specific effort to exercise human intelligence to understand the order of things. Moreover, the thing which these studies produce is understanding, which is not a physical object.

The Son is the *logos* of all creation. The Son gives rational order to everything that is made, as we have seen in our discussion of how the Trinity creates ("Why do we believe in the Trinity?"). The Son also provides us with the intellectual capacity to understand something of how creation works and how God works in and through it. The Son, therefore, is present in and to everybody. We do not bring Christ to anyone; Christ is already present in everyone whom we meet. The Son gives meaning to creation. The Son gives us the ability to understand something of that meaning. The Son also explains creation to us; this is one of the reasons for the Incarnation of the Son in Jesus the Christ. Thus, we turn to a discussion of the Incarnation.

2. What is the significance of Jesus's birth?

The Incarnation (the technical term for God's taking on humanity in Jesus) is consistent with God's choice to create, rather than being a radical departure from a pre-existing game plan. The conception and birth of Jesus is a world-transforming event, establishing a unity between God and creation. That is why both Matthew and Luke, who give us the accounts of Jesus's birth, emphasize that the child is the offspring of the Holy Spirit and a woman. Both Gospels also use titles for Jesus that emphasize the meeting of God and humanity: in Matthew, an angel calls Jesus "Emmanuel," which means "God is with us" (Matthew 1:23); and in Luke an angel calls Jesus "the Messiah" (which means the same as "the Christ" – anointed one) and "the Lord," which implies that the author of Luke understands Jesus as being somehow one with the Father. John's Prologue again provides the clearest assertion of the Incarnation as God entering into history, "and the Word became flesh and lived among us, and we have seen his glory, the glory as of a father's only son, full of grace and truth" (John 1:14).

What is the nature of this unity between God and creation? How can God and creation be united without them becoming one thing, in which both lose themselves? This is the heart of the question that the church debated for the first 400+ years of its existence (see: "How did the Christian understanding of God develop?"). The church's conclusions come in two parts: (1) there is a transformation in creation through humanity, whereby we become something greater than we were, as a consequence of the Incarnation; and (2) Jesus Christ must have possessed two complete natures, one divine and one human, for this to be possible.

People often think of the Incarnation as a divine rescue mission, triggered by the human decision to sin rather than staying true to God's plan for us. This is the argument of *Cur Deus Homo – Why God Became Man* – which is the explanation of the Incarnation that has been most influential in forming Reformation-era and modern Western theology. (It was written by Anselm in 1098.) Such an understanding is merely partial. The Incarnation answers the problem introduced by sin, but Christ's work is much more than that.

The Incarnation has two primary consequences: (1) God and creation are united; and (2) God reveals Godself to us. The unity of God and creation is tremendously important. This union transforms all of the created order, by elevating creation into something greater than its natural capacities would allow it to become. In the Incarnation, God takes on all aspects of creation: the physical, material stuff – complete with its ability to grow and change – that we share with all of the material creation, including the simplest forms of life; the capacities of feeling, willing and acting that we share with all other animals; and the ability to reason, with all of its attendant imaginative and reflective aspects, that we possess as humans. The last of these, the ability to reason, is the most complex aspect of creation that we know about; it is what gives humanity its tremendous impact on the world. God assumes (the traditional word for "taking on") all of the characteristics which we have listed and transforms them, making us able to be suitable partners for God. This is eternal life; it is life in which we participate in God's life, rather than being limited to life as defined by our own natural capacities.

God cannot change. The unity of divine and human natures does not undermine Christ's divinity, so the Son cannot change. Creatures can change, however; indeed, if we are to participate in God's life, then we need to do so. The impact of this meeting of divine and human on humanity and all creation is profound. We receive something of God's ability to love God and our neighbour, which is the true fulfilment of the life of all creation. From this love, all joy flows. We become a new creation.

Moreover, because God is eternal and all of God's actions have eternal implications, the Incarnation affects everyone, everywhere and at all times. Have you ever been bothered by the question of how God saves people who lived before the birth of Jesus the Christ? Or people who have had no opportunity of hearing about God and God's saving work? The answer is that God works with them just as God does with you and me. All of us are reached by the power of the Incarnation. All of history is transformed and given its true meaning in the Incarnation.

Part of the joy of life, though, is in knowing that God is doing this, that God loves us and wants us to share in God's love. The Incarnation is the revelation of God, because the Son is the exact representation of the Father. "And the Word became flesh and lived among us, and we have seen his glory, the glory as of a father's only son, full of grace and truth" (John 1:14 – "the glory of the Father's only Son" is also a legitimate reading of the text). As Jesus says, in John 14:7, "If you know me, you will know my Father also. From now on you do know him and have seen him." Jesus shows us what God is like and enables us to understand God's loving intention for the creation that God is making. He is "the true light, which enlightens everyone" (John 1:9), reaching out to everyone with God's good news. This good news is that God has transformed history and is building God's Reign in the created order. This is the secret of life; to delve into it more deeply requires that we talk about the life of Jesus the Christ, which we will do in further sections.

3. How can Jesus be fully divine and fully human?

Our lengthy discussion of Jesus's birth raises a question: "If Jesus Christ is fully God, then how can he truly live as a man, sharing our manifest limitations, though not our sinfulness?" This is a complicated question that cannot be completely answered. Only the eternal God can fully explain the union of divine and human – and we probably could not understand the answer anyway. Because we are not eternal and are not really capable of understanding what being eternal is like, this is a question which is, in principle, beyond the capacities of our intellect.

That is not, however, the whole answer, because theologians have been able to clarify the situation somewhat. The Incarnation is not an obscure doctrine, though it is a bit complicated. We begin with a rather tantalizing word that the Apostle Paul gave us. In his letter to the Christians at Philippi, Paul (probably quoting a contemporary hymn) says,

> Let the same mind be in you that was in Christ Jesus,
> who, though he was in the form of God,
> did not regard equality with God
> as something to be exploited, but emptied himself,
> taking the form of a slave.
> And being found in human form,
> he humbled himself
> and became obedient to the point of death –
> even death on a cross. (Philippians 2:6–8)

The Greek for "emptied himself" is *kenosis*. It gives rise to "kenotic Christology," which focuses upon this issue of divine self-limitation.

While *"kenosis"* can be interpreted in a variety of ways, the root issue is really quite simple; it is a problem of proportionality. If God, in Jesus the Christ, did not act in a way that respected the humanity of Jesus, then God would have undermined God's own aims. A simple analogy might help. Assume that you are driving a Ferrari (I know . . . you wish!) on the way to an appointment, for which you are late. Your route leads you, unavoidably, past a large primary school at letting-out time. You have two options: (1) use all of your Ferrari's potential, blowing past the school at racetrack speeds, in an effort to reach your appointment on time; or (2) slow down to the indicated speed limit, paying careful attention to every child on or near the roadway. If you need to think about which option to choose, then I strongly encourage you to run (on foot) to your nearest Department of Motor Vehicles office and surrender your driving permit, immediately. Option 1 is very likely to involve you in accidents, deaths and police intervention, preventing you from fulfilling the goal of reaching the appointment at any time, in addition to wreaking great destruction of life and property. Only option 2 will enable you to accomplish your intended purpose whilst also serving the common good. Applying all of the Ferrari's power to solve the difficulty would amount to a disproportionate use of force, which would be self-defeating.

Similarly, as we have seen in prior discussion ("What do we mean when we speak of God as 'eternal'?"), God does not need to think about God's options, since God does only the right thing under every circumstance. Consequently, God's actions must always be proportionate to the intended purpose. If God acted in a manner completely disproportionate to the human capacity to sustain, then God could not reveal Godself in Jesus the Christ. This is simply consistent with every other divine action; all of them are precisely measured to suit their goals. God is not a blundering giant, wandering around and whacking every problem with an oversized club; God is much more subtle than that.

In Jesus the Christ, then, God retains full Godness; this is not really quantifiable and cannot be lost or stripped away. The divine nature acts in a manner consistent with divine nature. It leads the human nature, reveals itself to it and transforms it to the precise degree needed to accomplish God's purpose. To do otherwise would be a real loss of Godhood. The Jesus with whom the disciples interacted, therefore, displayed his full, but transformed, humanity. This was not overwhelmed and destroyed by his divinity. On the other hand, the disciples and others encountered a person charged with the divine power needed to fulfil the divine mission of establishing the Reign of God, showing forth its nature and announcing his power over it.

The culmination of this manifestation of divinity in partnership with humanity in Jesus the Christ occurs at the moment of the Transfiguration. This story appears in Matthew 17:1–13, Mark 9:2–13, Luke 9:28–36, and 2 Peter 1:16–18. Jesus takes several of his disciples, Peter, James and John, up a great mountain. While they are at the top, Jesus's appearance changes – he is "transfigured before them," his face shines like the sun and his clothes become dazzling white. He is speaking with Moses and Elijah. A voice comes from heaven, saying, "This is my Son, the Beloved; with him I am well pleased; listen to him" (Matthew 17:5). The disciples encounter Jesus in a way different from any that have come before. In fear, they fall down and hide their eyes. Jesus tells them to get up and let go of their fear. When they do so, Jesus is alone.

Jesus does not seem to be at all surprised by what happens. There is no evidence that he thinks of this as a change in himself or his status. Instead, this appears to be a change in the way that the disciples view Jesus. They meet him as a heavenly one, with heavenly attestation. He communes with the great leaders and prophets of Israel's past, who also have prophetic connections to Israel's future. Jesus is revealed as one who is a full participant in the heavenly realm. Indeed, the Father speaks of Jesus as his Son and Beloved, pointing to the intimate relationship between the Father and Jesus, the Son of God. In conversation afterward, Jesus speaks of himself as "the Son of Man" and reminds the disciples that he will suffer at the hands of worldly authorities, thereby emphasizing that he is also the human who defines humanity.

In this conjunction, we meet the one Jesus who brings together the divine and the human. We are also reminded of his firm sense of mission and his refusal to depart from it. This sense of divine mission defines the life of Jesus among us, which is why we will discuss it next.

4. How does Jesus's life serve the Reign of God?

When he [Jesus] came to Nazareth, where he had been brought up, he went to the synagogue on the sabbath day, as was his custom. He stood up to read, and the scroll of the prophet Isaiah was given to him. He unrolled the scroll and found the place where it was written:

> "The Spirit of the Lord is upon me,
> because he has anointed me to bring good news to the poor.
> He has sent me to proclaim release to the captives
> and recovery of sight to the blind,
> to let the oppressed go free,
> to proclaim the year of the Lord's favor."

And he rolled up the scroll, gave it back to the attendant, and sat down. The eyes of all in the synagogue were fixed on him. Then he began to say to them, "Today this scripture has been fulfilled in your hearing." (Luke 4:16–21)

This dramatic story gets to the heart of Jesus's life and its significance to us. Jesus is a sacrament, which is a visible and material sign of God's grace (you can see it and feel it) that effects what it signifies (it causes to happen the same thing which it announces). Jesus travels around telling people about the Reign of God. He supports this announcement with acts that demonstrate the presence of the Reign, culminating in his own resurrection and ascension, which we will discuss in other sections ("What is the significance of Jesus's resurrection?" and "What is the significance of Jesus's ascension?"). Jesus also calls us to participate in God's Reign, by knowing and living in the love which God shows in creating and transforming everything.

For those accustomed to other language, I should begin by noting that the phrase "Reign of God" means the same as "kingdom of God" and "kingdom of heaven." In all of these terms the word "Reign" or "kingdom" is *basileia*, which refers to that place where the ruler's will is done, where the ruler directs and is obeyed. "Reign" or "kingdom" of God simply states that this is where God rules. "kingdom of heaven" says that this is where the one who lives in heaven rules; we imply something similar when we say "Heaven knows!," indicating that we do not know the answer to a question – only God knows.

Jesus's preaching has three basic characteristics: (1) it announces the coming of the Reign of God; (2) it indicates what that Reign is like; and (3) it calls people to live in the Reign of God. In the Gospels, we often see Jesus communicating in parables. Parables can be difficult to understand, in part because the term "parable" covers a variety of sayings. In addition, parables are often ambiguous. Stories do not usually have univocal morals or implications; even where a moral is stated, the listener or reader may find many other possible lessons in the story and some of those lessons may be profoundly opposed to the meaning intended. Parables, which often are stories, share that openness to interpretation. They may be read with the greatest understanding of history, context and language, and still present recipients with a variety of possible meanings.

The most obvious function of parables is to link the Reign of God to the contemporary world, to familiar situations and circumstances. This is a way of heralding the coming of the Reign and hinting at its character. "The kingdom of heaven is like yeast that a woman took and mixed in with three measures of flour until all of it was leavened" (Matthew 13:33; also Luke 13:20–21). That is the whole story; no moral is drawn. The reader is left to extract meaning from the symbolic comparison. In the context of all of Jesus's words, we can interpret the simile as suggesting that God is like the baking woman; God takes all of the actions which participate in God's Reign and mixes them in with every other action. Such actions have a transforming and elevating effect upon the world, causing it all to become the world which God wants it to be. This is, of course, only one interpretation; others are possible. The parable causes us to think about the Reign of God, however, and focus upon the way in which the world around us might be seen in its light. This helps to make us people of God's Reign.

Jesus also uses more direct forms of speech, including lengthy sermons. These are helpful, both because they can be useful in explaining the more elliptical sayings of the parables and because they tend to include explicit comments on the nature of life in the Reign of God.

Perhaps the most famous sermon is what most people call "The Sermon on the Mount," because the Gospel of Matthew describes it as happening on a mountain (Matthew 5:1–12; it also appears in Luke 6:20–23). According to this sermon, the Reign of God is a reign of divine, and therefore loving, justice. In it, the poor and the meek, the hungry and the sad, will find blessing and comfort. In it, those who want to be good will find goodness, the merciful will receive mercy, the peacemakers will know God's peace, and those who have committed their lives to God will know God. In it, the unjustly persecuted find their reward.

The rest of Jesus's preaching has this same character, raising up the downtrodden and cutting down the great, as is suggested in the passage with which this section began. Jesus proclaimed divine justice and announced the "year of the Lord's favour," which is the Year of Jubilee. The Jubilee year, commanded in Leviticus 25, was expected to occur every 50 years. Servants were to be freed from their indentures; most properties which had been sold were to be returned to their previous owners, so that everyone could return to their ancestral lands; debts were to be cancelled. This was intended to be a time when the weakest and poorest of society received a fresh chance and the richest and most powerful were required to be generous. Probably, it never occurred. However, Jesus's choice to associate himself with the Year of Jubilee, as its proclaimer, makes clear his understanding of the Reign of God. Jubilee is a radical re-ordering of the world, in which the downtrodden are raised up.

Wandering around saying such nice things sounds like rather a kind activity, a good way to inject a bit of joy into the life of people who have had a rough time of it. However, Jesus the Christ does not content himself with *preaching* good news to the poor; instead, he *brings* good news to the poor. This becomes evident from the very beginning of the gospel story. Indeed, in Luke's Gospel, Mary celebrates the coming of the Reign of God in her song of joy, even before Jesus is born.

My soul magnifies the Lord, and my spirit rejoices in God my Savior,
for he has looked with favor on the lowliness of his servant.
Surely, from now on all generations will call me blessed;
for the Mighty One has done great things for me,
and holy is his name.

His mercy is for those who fear him from generation to generation.
He has shown strength with his arm;
he has scattered the proud in the thoughts of their hearts.
He has brought down the powerful from their thrones, and lifted up the lowly;
he has filled the hungry with good things, and has sent the rich away empty.
He has helped his servant Israel, in remembrance of his mercy, according to the promise he made to our ancestors,
to Abraham and to his descendants forever. (Luke 1:47–55)

This is clearly a hymn and it was probably in use in the early church; certainly, it is used that way today. I suspect that many people have sung it without listening very carefully to the radical vision of justice and the Reign of God which it declares. Mary begins by declaring her own low status in the world; an ordinary young woman who is pregnant while not yet married is not an impressive figure in her day and age. Then she begins to generalize, announcing that God works in and through those who are not in high esteem in their societies; God gives power to the powerless and food to the hungry. At the same time, God takes away power from the strong and refuses to serve the rich. In all of this, God fulfils the ancient promises to Israel. This is the Reign of God. This is what Jesus the Christ was born to inaugurate.

We have discussed the Incarnation, in which God takes on humanity and, in doing so, adopts all aspects of creation. In doing so, God takes on the weakness and fragility of created life and transforms it. This is the elevation of that which is valuable only to God. Yet God makes us very like Godself (the point made in Psalm 8:5 and Hebrews 2:7) and gives us true life and great responsibility. Moreover, God does this as the son of ordinary people, instead of choosing to use a royal person.

We see Jesus the Christ caring for and empowering the outcasts of society in many ways. Sometimes it is with a show of kindness to them which, simultaneously, rebukes the powerful and apparently righteous. The story of a woman caught in adultery is an example of this. In John 8:3–11, the Pharisees (religious and political leaders with a very strict moral code) bring the woman to Jesus and point out that the law demands that her crime be punished by stoning. They want to know what Jesus believes to be appropriate for her. He says, "Let anyone among you who is without sin be the first to throw a stone at her." Then he bends down and writes in the sand with his finger. The supposedly-righteous people who brought her to Jesus vanish. Jesus straightens up and asks the woman whether anyone has condemned her. She tells him that no-one has. His response is: "Neither do I condemn you. Go your way and from now on do not sin again." Thus, she is freed from an unhealthy life and its consequences, while those in authority who would condemn her – feeling safe in their sense of their own righteousness – are publicly shamed.

Jesus also raises up the lowly with his acts of power. These acts teach, as well as causing physical transformation. They are of a piece with the sermon in which Jesus blesses the poor and meek, and the parables in which the Reign of God is shown to those who wish to see it. He heals the sick (e.g. Matthew 8:14–17; Mark 1:29–34; Luke 4:38–41) and blind (for example, Matthew 20:29–34; Mark 10:46–52; Luke 18:35–43). He touches and cleanses a man stricken with leprosy, a term for skin diseases which characterized the true outcasts of the ancient world – lepers had to live outside the city, so that they would not infect others (Matthew 8:1–4; Mark 1:40–45; Luke 5:12–16). The list goes on ... Often, the act of power is attached to some sort of proclamation, as in the healing of the paralysed man, which includes a declaration of Jesus's power over the sin which infects the earth and is followed by people glorifying God (Matthew 9:2–8; Mark 2:1–12; Luke 5:17–26). This proclamation is important, because it leads to an important part of Jesus's ministry: the call.

We have said that Jesus the Christ is the light of the world, the one who shows God's face in the world. However, the light does not stop at its source.

You are the light of the world. A city built on a hill cannot be hid. No one after lighting a lamp puts it under the bushel basket, but on the lampstand, and it gives light to all in the house. In the same way, let your light shine before others, so that they may

see your good works and give glory to your Father in heaven.
(Matthew 5:14–16)

Jesus gives the light to us and calls upon us to convey it to the
world. How can we do that when we are not God? We can live
eternal life, which means living God's life. "Love your enemies
and pray for those who persecute you, so that you may be children
of your Father in heaven" (Matthew 5:44–45). Find the humility
and sensitivity of children; live in it and share it with children
(Matthew 18:1–7; Mark 9:37; Luke 17:1–2). "Proclaim the
kingdom of God and heal" (Luke 9:2) Above all, serve the poor
and needy. God does not distinguish people according to their
earthly status, but on the basis of whether they feed the hungry;
give drink to the thirsty; welcome the stranger; clothe the naked;
or visit the sick and the imprisoned (Matthew 25:31–46).

We are called to live the life which Jesus lives and preach what
Jesus preaches; this is the implication of being adopted into God's
family. The point of the Incarnation is precisely that it transforms
us into the kind of people who can recognize the Reign of God,
announce it and live it. It transforms the world into the kind of
place where the Reign of God can flourish. However, just as the
destruction wrought by our efforts to oppose God's Reign continually makes itself known in our lives, so it interferes with the life
of Jesus the Christ. We kill him.

5. Why did Jesus die?

Christians have puzzled over the meaning of Jesus's death since it
happened. It appears to make no sense, especially from the point-
of-view of the earliest believers. If Jesus had been the presence of
God among them, establishing the Reign of God, then his ugly
death at the hands of Roman soldiers pushed by a mob hungry for
spectacle is altogether out of place. It all seems so pointless and
depressing, even scary. After his resurrection, though, people begin
to find clues to the meaning of his death in things that he had said
and in the Jewish tradition which formed him.

The Gospel of Mark is centered on Jesus's movement toward his death. The pivotal moment in Mark comes in chapter 8, starting at verse 27, with Jesus's announcement of what will happen to him. He quizzes the disciples about who other people think that he is – and then about their own understanding of him. The climactic moment comes when Peter announces that Jesus is the Messiah. Jesus orders them to keep this secret and begins to lecture them about his future, with rejection, death and resurrection as its culmination. Characteristically for the disciples in Mark's Gospel, they do not understand at all. Peter tries to dissuade Jesus, but Jesus calls Peter "Satan" for his effort to deflect Jesus from the course which he must take. The gospel requires that one give up one's life to God's purposes, for only by doing so can one truly live. Next comes the Transfiguration and a swift movement toward the cross. In a sense, the Gospel of Mark often comes across as a crucifixion story with a prologue. Mark's focus upon Jesus's death causes us to ask about its significance for theology; Mark is probably the oldest Gospel and reflects the concern with which Christianity has viewed this death from the very beginning.

Thus, already in the biblical period, people are trying to understand what meaning, if any, Jesus's death might have for them. The evidence from Mark's Gospel suggests that commitment to God's purposes is the decisive consideration in Jesus's life – and must always be so for us. Jesus's death is an example of obedience to the divine will, which defines the true meaning of his life. This is especially evident through Jesus's prayer in the Garden of Gethsemane, when he shows a very human fear of the pain to come combined with a clear submission to God's will (Mark 14:32–42; Matthew 26:36–46; Luke 22:39–46). In the face of all the powers of his society, Jesus always holds firm.

The biblical documents have more to say about the importance of Jesus's death. Very quickly, the followers of Jesus come to regard it as sacrificial, a death which somehow occurs on their behalf. This understanding has an intricate relationship with Jewish thought and history. The language of "death" and "blood" become a way of distinguishing Jesus's followers from other strands of Jewish religion and, ultimately, from Judaism generally. Even as Judaism was about to move away from blood sacrifice, Christianity was coming into being as a religion that declared such sacrifice to be unnecessary.

Paul speaks of Jesus as "a sacrifice of atonement" who justifies us (Romans 3:25) and reconciles us to God (Romans 5:6–11). This usage is intended to emphasize the freedom that we receive through Christ. In Hebrew religion, the sacrifice of atonement was given annually as a sign of readiness to be reconciled to God, a plea to God for forgiveness of sin and re-establishment of right relationship (Leviticus 23:26–32; Numbers 29:7–11). Paul argues that sin no longer has us in its grip, for Christ reconciles us to God. Instead, we must live the life of faith, through the power of the Holy Spirit; we must trust in God's love for our salvation and look forward to the completion of God's Reign (Romans 8). We must live the life of Christ, being Christ's body in and to the world (Romans 12:1–15:6). Doing so enables us to share in Christ's death and resurrection, which we enter into through baptism (Romans 6:1–14). Paul picks up the symbolism of blood and sacrifice from his Jewish heritage, but does so only to break its power. The point of his argument is that Jesus's followers can use the Jewish symbols, but Christ has freed people from Jewish law (Romans 2:17–29).

The Letter to the Hebrews (author unknown) says something similar, in an exceedingly technical argument that hinges on an understanding of traditional Jewish law. The purpose of the discussion is to convince Jewish followers of Jesus that they need not continue to make the sacrifices which Jewish law requires; instead, these people must persevere in the new and living way, focusing upon "love and good deeds" and meeting together (Hebrews 10:19–39). Jesus, the Son, is "the reflection of God's glory and the exact imprint of God's very being" (Hebrews 1:3) and is faithful in creating and ruling the world as God's Son must be (Hebrews 3:1–6). Jesus has become the sacrifice which cleanses us and makes us holy (Hebrews 9:15–10:18), so that no more sacrifices are necessary. He is forever and so is the impact of his self-sacrifice (Hebrews 7:23).

Moreover, Jesus is "the high priest" in a defining and ultimate sense (Hebrews 2:14–18). The high priest is the leading performer of sacrificial acts in the Jewish context. Jesus gives his own life; it is not taken from him by any human power. His faithfulness to the

Father is God's faithfulness. Thus, Jesus is the divine high priest who does not need to make any offering for sin, but he accepts death out of obedience. Instead of fighting or running, Jesus stands for the Reign of God until the end. In the process, he establishes a new covenant which is built upon faithfulness to God (Hebrews 8; also 10:15–18) and provides an example of the meaning of true faith (Hebrews 12:1–12). We need not be afraid of God, but may expect mercy and aid from God (Hebrew 4:16). Our focus must be on the life of faith and love (Hebrews 10–13), as we look forward to the completion of God's Reign and the rest which it brings (Hebrews 4:1–13).

We are not especially concerned with the task of separating ourselves from the practices of mid-1st-century Judaism, so that large parts of the argument made in Paul's writings and Hebrews are not relevant to our lives. However, some important points are made in the biblical reflections on Jesus's death. Humanity commits evil, but God takes the evil and transforms it. Moreover, the greatest evil which humanity could commit is the means by which God performs that transformation. Killing Jesus is a human act, but only by Jesus's choice to be obedient to the Father could it occur. Jesus refuses to fight or run; instead, he stands up for the Reign of God until the end. His death is consistent with all other parts of his life. As Paul says, "Being found in human form, he humbled himself and became obedient to the point of death – even death on a cross" (Philippians 2:8). The biblical writers are definite in their belief that Jesus has both the power and the righteousness necessary to avoid this death. He accepts it because the mission of God's Reign requires it. To avoid death would demand that Jesus renounce God's way and accept the way of self-interest; he must stop preaching, teaching, and performing works of power. This is not possible for him.

Consequently, Jesus's death becomes an example for his followers, demonstrating true obedience to the Father's will. It is more than just an example to be emulated, however; the death itself begins a transformation in the nature of the world, a change that will be completed in the resurrection and ascension. The death, therefore, becomes part of the symbol of new life into which Christians enter in the sacrament of baptism. It becomes an integral part of the life of faith. Trusting in God, we are called to show forth God's love; doing so makes us sacraments of God's Reign to the world, as we look forward to the fulfilment of God's Reign.

Reflection on the meaning of Jesus's death did not end when the Bible was composed. Some early Christian thinkers developed the "ransom" theory to describe what they understood Jesus's death to accomplish. According to this theory, Jesus died to free humanity from the evil powers that enslave us. The death of a truly innocent person functions as payment, to buy our freedom. Anselm, a medieval thinker, rejects this theory; it seems to imply that some other power can own us and force God to pay for us. This idea dishonours God. Anselm's answer is that our sin incurs a debt of honour to God, because we owe God absolute fealty. In other words, our task is always to do God's will; any failure to do so takes away something from God which belongs to God. Instead of forcing us to suffer because we cannot ever repay this debt (remember, we have nothing that we do not owe to God), God pays the debt by becoming incarnate and dying. This death is the only work in history in which God is given something that was not owed (the technical definition of a "work of super-erogation") and it covers all debts that we might possibly incur against God. Anselm's theory is called a "penal substitutionary atonement" theory, because Jesus pays a penalty (penal) on our behalf (substitutionary) in order to make us one with God (at-one-ment, but pronounced a-tone-ment).

Another way of understanding Jesus's death became popular in the 18th, 19th and 20th centuries. It combines the biblical language of blood with later theories, in ways that can be quite gruesome. The essence of the argument is that Jesus's blood buys our freedom (a sacrifice which pays a ransom) and washes us clean of sin (making us holy). This approach is evident in a whole generation of hymns, which proclaim sentiments like: "There is a fountain filled with blood, drawn from Emmanuel's veins. And sinners washed beneath that flood lose all their guilty stains" (William Cowper, 1772).

Theologians since Anselm have found all of these theories to be unsatisfactory. Anselm was right to criticize the ransom theory; there is no other power in the universe which can demand a ransom from God. However, Anselm's own approach seems to suggest either that God's honour is something independent of God, which is absurd, or that God has to pay God to make the cosmos unfold as it ought to, which seems unnecessary. And the bloody language of some recent efforts is simply disgusting, without clarifying how Jesus's death might be helpful to us.

From the human vantage point, death never really makes sense; this is especially true of the premature death of the innocent. We see precisely what the disciples saw: great possibilities cut off before they could be fulfilled. Undoubtedly, God sees in such a situation the opportunity to act redemptively in people's lives, since this is how God acts under all circumstances. However, we go to tremendous lengths to keep ourselves alive, often coming close to forgetting that too extreme a commitment to saving our lives will cost us life.

That is Jesus's point: people who hang on to their own lives to the exclusion of all other considerations will lose life (Mark 8:35). Instead, Jesus calls us to a life of faithfulness to God, to an unceasing effort to live the Reign of God. That is what causes Jesus's death. He does not die because he is born with a suicide mission to pay off God or some malevolent cosmic power. He dies because the earthly powers see him as a disruptive influence, upsetting delicate diplomatic balances and re-ordering the social, political and religious world. He is killed because some people are so busy trying to maintain their own lives, their own powers, that they cannot see the Reign of God. They know that Jesus proclaims himself to be a king, but they do not know what he ruled (and rules). Strange as it may seem, Jesus's death is a gift of life to us, because it declares that the Reign of God transcends our own self-centeredness. All of those life considerations which dominate our time are really secondary; if they become the primary meanings of our lives, then we die. Real life is found in true faithfulness to God; it is the life of the Reign of God.

And it may cost us our lives . . .

6. What is the significance of Jesus's resurrection?

Death is not the end of Jesus's story, however. Instead, Jesus's life culminates in victory over death, as he rises from the tomb and reveals himself to his followers. Then, he ascends into heaven. To many people, all of this sounds rather like a fairy tale, necessary only because it provides a happy ending for what would otherwise be a tragedy. To Christians, however, the resurrection and ascension are important because of their impact on daily life. They are part of the sacrament which is Jesus the Christ, symbols which cause what they signify. In this case, they signify the salvation that God in Christ has built into the structure of creation.

The stories of the risen Jesus have him appearing to his disciples and giving them final directions. These narratives appear to have three basic points to make: (1) death has now been defeated, because Jesus is alive; (2) he really is alive, in a recognizable body which can do extraordinary things while yet being capable of eating and being touched; and (3) Jesus intends to found the church, as a bodily continuation of the work of the Reign of God on earth.

Like the Incarnation, the resurrection is an eternal action, with consequences for all of history. It gives structure and meaning to the created order. Jesus's resurrection announces that death does not have the final word. Instead, God brings new life out of death.

This is the way that the world works; out of every form of destruction, God brings something new. When something dies, God incorporates it into a new thing. We can see this at the most basic of levels in creation; even the component parts of rocks and trees are continually reused. However, resurrection means something different for humans. (It may also mean more for other creatures, animate or inanimate; that is not for me to say. I speak only for humans, because I know a little about them.) For us, resurrection is not only about conservation of energy, whereby the matter of which we are composed continues to be used by the universe. Resurrection has physical, intellectual and spiritual components, which we experience in daily life and look forward to.

As I write this, I sit at my desk in the pre-dawn darkness. I think about the things that I will do today. In a couple of hours, I will roust my children from their beds, encourage them to get dressed for school, and prepare breakfast for them. In each of these activities, I may be an agent of God's resurrection or I may be an agent of destruction. I may contribute to my children's growth or impede it. Which I will do is dependent in part upon the amount of care that I am willing to bring to the task; if I am prepared to give my loving attention to my sons, employing the best of my spiritual and intellectual resources to serve the work of caring for them, then I stand a better chance of participating in the new life that God is forming in them. Although I have limited knowledge and ability in this (and every other!) area, God honours my efforts and incorporates them into the lives of my children. This is part of the good news.

Parents will recognize that this beautiful vision has a tendency not to materialize as often as we wish. For various reasons, we find ourselves behaving with our children in ways that we do not like. We find ourselves distracted when we want to be attentive, angry when we want to be calm, yelling when we want to speak gently. This is a consequence of our own failure to do what we ought to do; our children's failure to do what they ought to do; and the general limitedness of humanity which causes us to work at cross-purposes. Another part of the good news is that God still works new life in us and our children. God takes our failures and brings good out of them, just as God does with our successes. This is the doctrine of redemption, about which more will be said in the section on salvation ("What is redemption?").

God's activity of bringing good out of our destructive actions is also a consequence of the resurrection. Humanity undertakes to do the greatest evil it can manage, in murdering Jesus. God's response is the resurrection; Jesus the Christ returns from the dead to announce that God overcomes whatever evil we commit. Destruction cannot win.

Resurrection also has a future component for us. Human beings tend to be future-oriented; we live our days with one eye on tomorrow. Resurrection is part of the Christian answer to what will happen in the future. The Apostle Paul describes Jesus as "the firstfruits of those who have died," arguing that Jesus's resurrection both announces and enables the resurrection of dead humanity.

Paul is asserting that physical death is not the end for us. This is consistent with Jesus's own promise of resurrection for all (for example, John 5:19–29). Paul also makes the point that the life that we look forward to after death does not merely consist of a vague kind of floating around of some sort of essence; Paul does not defend a doctrine of the immortality of the soul (common in some philosophical traditions that are built around Platonic metaphysics). Instead, Paul argues that our resurrected bodies will be like that which Jesus the Christ took on, for we will "bear the image of the man of heaven" (1 Corinthians 15:49). Christians take belief in the resurrection of the body very seriously; we reassert our commitment to this doctrine every time that we say the Apostles' Creed or the Nicene Creed.

This is not, however, the only meaning of the language of "the body of Christ," for Paul. Paul often speaks of the church as "the body of Christ" (e.g. 1 Corinthians 12:12). Throughout Jesus's ministry, we can see evidence that he is training the disciples to continue his work in the world, so that it will continue when Jesus is not physically present. He is constantly showing the Reign of God to the disciples, while telling them how to further it. Remember that the Gospels were written after Jesus's death; they were composed by and for communities of Jesus's followers.

However, the post-resurrection appearance stories seem to be particularly focused on commissioning and building up the church. Matthew ends with Jesus sending out the disciples, commissioning them to baptize "in the name of the Father and of the Son and of the Holy Spirit" and teaching them; Matthew also reminds the church of Jesus's continuing presence with his people (Matthew 28:16–20). Mark is a complicated case, because ancient texts have different endings. The earlier ending happens rather abruptly, while the second ending is similar to Matthew's (though without the Triune name). John concludes with Jesus giving the gift of a special presence of the Holy Spirit to the disciples (John 20:22) and a comment on church leadership, presented as an explanation of Peter's authority. Three times, Jesus asks Peter whether Peter loves him. When Peter responds affirmatively, Jesus tells him to care for the flock, using sheep metaphors. One who loves Jesus must show that love to others and true leadership consists in demonstrating that love to the community. Jesus follows this discussion with a prophecy that Peter will be crucified, as Jesus was, suggesting that church leadership is sacrificial; it is not about sparing the self, but about serving the Reign of God in the world. Then, Jesus concludes with the simple command which is at the root of his call to the first disciples and to the world today: "Follow me" (John 21:15–19).

The most church-oriented of endings, however, is certainly Luke's. The best available evidence suggests that the author of Luke also wrote what we call "The Acts of the Apostles" (which might more accurately be called "Some Acts of Some Apostles," in recognition that it is not the whole story). Luke concludes with two of Jesus's followers walking along a road; a man appears to them and explains the story of Jesus to them. All three sit down to supper. When the bread is broken, the two recognize Jesus as their companion. Indeed, this is the story that they pass on to the disciples and others: they talk about how Jesus had been made known to them "in the breaking of the bread" (Luke 24:13–35). This is evidently intended to be a eucharistic story; it is the kind of story that the early church would have used as a reminder that they meet Jesus in the eucharistic service. This is a resurrection story that reflects the heart of the church's life.

After this, Jesus appears to the disciples and tells them to stay in Jerusalem until they have been "clothed with power from on high" (Luke 24:36–49). The opening of Acts begins with the ascension of Jesus and the church's empowering with the Holy Spirit, so we will move to discussing these matters.

7. What is the significance of Jesus's ascension?

This is one of those miraculous stories that inspires scepticism in the reader. Only Luke-Acts gives us a real ascension story; the second ending of Mark's Gospel is the most helpful other source and it tells us only that Jesus "was taken up into heaven and sat down at the right hand of God" (Mark 16:19). The more complete account is in Acts, which tells us that Jesus promised the disciples that they would receive the power of the Holy Spirit, enabling them to serve as witnesses to Jesus and the Reign of God, and then,

> when he had said this, as they were watching, he was lifted up, and a cloud took him out of their sight. While he was going and they were gazing up toward heaven, suddenly two men in white robes stood by them. They said, "Men of Galilee, why do you stand looking up toward heaven? This Jesus, who has been taken up from you into heaven, will come in the same way as you saw him go into heaven. (Acts 1:6–11)

We have, of course, no way of knowing whether the disciples saw what they thought they saw. Certainly, from the perspective of the narrative, this is a useful conclusion to the Jesus story. It is much more satisfying than simply ending with a resurrection appearance and no real departure. Moreover, the spectacle of Jesus rising into a cloud and not returning, while theologically unnecessary because God is equally present everywhere, is symbolically helpful. In a world that tends to use the metaphor of "above" for God and heaven, having Jesus rise into the Father's presence makes sense. There is precedence in the Hebrew story for such a happening, and the disciples would have been familiar with it: Elijah did something similar, although his ascension in a fiery chariot is much more dramatic (2 Kings 2:1–12). Consequently, there is a logic to the assertion that Jesus made an exit of the kind described in Acts; such an action would have communicated the idea that he was leaving the physical, earthly realm, and entering into whatever follows, more vividly than words ever could.

The problem for us, though, is in knowing what to do with such a story. Is it anything more than special effects, 1st-century style? The first consequence of the ascension is to switch the focus. Luke uses it to shift our eyes from Jesus, walking around on earth, to Jesus completing the Reign of God (I know that the language of Jesus "coming again" is troublesome for many people; we will discuss it in the section on salvation – see "What do we mean when we talk about 'Christ's return'?"). We are turned to face the future. This is precisely what the disciples immediately do. They meet together and choose a replacement for Judas (Acts 1:12–26).

This is a statement of firm determination; the community is now formed and is preparing itself for the work of God's Reign. The ascension, thus, serves as a link between: (1) Jesus's earthly ministry; (2) the work of the church; and (3) the fulfilment of the purpose of all creation in the Reign of God. The ascension is a defining point in Christian life, because it helps us to look backward to Jesus, around ourselves at our present task, and forward to the hope which gives ultimate meaning to transient accomplishments.

The ascension also tells us something about the nature of our salvation. The natural inclination of the disciples is to stand around staring upward, wondering what has happened. This leads to sore necks; it does not lead to sanctification. Commitment to the Reign of God means a forward movement, following Jesus into the future. It means a genuine willingness to do what God asks, as we travel through life. However, the disciples were not altogether wrong to "think upwards." Entering into God's life, which is the life of the Reign of God, is a kind of elevation for us. The ascension serves as a kind of symbolic representation of this. There is a sense in which the work of the Holy Spirit within us enables us to transcend the limitations of our nature. As we live and work, performing the most mundane of tasks, God brings us into the divine presence. In order to understand what all this means, we shall think about salvation. First, however, we must discuss the Holy Spirit.

Who is the Holy Spirit?

The Holy Spirit is the giver of life, the one who calls forth a response to the Christ, God's creating, redeeming, transforming Word. The Word is the divine self-expression, the proclamation of love within the Trinity and in the created order. Only that which is truly alive can respond in love. Within the Trinity, the Holy Spirit is the response-in-love. In the created order, the Holy Spirit acts to enable creation to provide the right response-in-love.

Thus, the Holy Spirit is the animating power of the created

order. The Hebrew word *ruach* and the Greek word *pneuma* both carry several meanings; "wind," "breath," and "spirit" are among them. Our understanding of the Holy Spirit, third person of the Trinity, is related to these multiple meanings.

The Bible contains two creation stories, appearing in Genesis 1:1–2:4a and 2:4b–3:24, respectively. The first creation story focuses upon the ordered coming-into-being of everything, while the second one emphasizes the making of humanity and our insistence upon doing things our way, rather than God's way. The first story begins with God's *ruach* sweeping over the waters (Genesis 1:2) and God calling creation into being. Creation happens through the speaking of God's Word, who is the Son, and the movement of God's Spirit, the Holy Spirit, into the created being. The Holy Spirit gives life to creation, in response to the speaking of God's Word. In the second creation story, God forms humanity from dust, the stuff of the earth. Then God breathes into our nostrils "the breath of life" and we become living beings (Genesis 2:7). Here, the Holy Spirit gives us our specific form of life; we do not live only as the earth lives, but are able to walk and talk, think and judge, decide and act. The breath of God is our breath.

However, Christians do not understand life as being limited to mere physical functioning. True life is eternal life, which is life in God. This is life lived in response to God's Word, who is the Christ. Thus, the Holy Spirit acts throughout the biblical stories, empowering various characters in the Hebrew Scriptures (Old Testament), as well as in the New Testament. Samson's strength (Judges 14:6) and Bezalel's "skill, intelligence, and knowledge in every kind of craft" (Exodus 35:31) come from the Spirit. Willingness to know God and follow God's way come from the Holy Spirit, as does the joy of life in God.

> Create in me a clean heart, O God,
> and put a new and right spirit within me.
> Do not cast me away from your presence,
> and do not take your holy spirit from me.
> Restore to me the joy of your salvation,
> and sustain in me a willing spirit. (Psalm 51:10–12)

In the Apocrypha (which may not appear in your Bible), the Spirit teaches us the wisdom that we need in order to do what God would have us do. The Holy Spirit provides us with both the knowledge and the ability necessary to live life in God.

Moreover, since true life is eternal life which comes through the Word, the Incarnation of the Son of God is at the centre of life. The activity of the Holy Spirit is integral to the Incarnation, in three distinct ways: (1) preparing the way, through prophetic announcements; (2) participating in the event itself and in the activity of Jesus the Christ; and (3) serving as the power going forth from the event and from all that Jesus the Christ said and did, to change the world.

The spirit of prophecy is the Holy Spirit; it enables the prophets to speak the divine word (e.g. Isaiah 59:21). The Holy Spirit, therefore, is the one who helps us to know what God is going to do. In an earlier section of this book, we noted that Jesus defined his own mission as bringing good news to the poor, proclaiming release to the captives and recovery of sight to the blind, letting the oppressed go free, and proclaiming the year of the Lord's favour (Luke 4:18–19). This is a quotation from a prophecy found in Isaiah 61. This prophecy emphasizes the Holy Spirit's role in bringing about the Reign of God, proclaimed by Jesus ("The spirit of the Lord God is upon me, because the Lord has anointed me" Isaiah 61:1). When Jesus is born among us, he does not merely fulfil some vague expectations which arose in the desperate conversations of a troubled people. Instead, Jesus is the fulfilment of a specific prophecy rooted in the activity of the Holy Spirit in the world.

The Gospels of Matthew and Luke focus on Jesus as the fulfilment of a Spirit-given prophecy. Luke surrounds the story of Jesus's birth with prophecies given through Zechariah, Simeon and Anna. The text explicitly declares that Zechariah was led by the Holy Spirit to prophesy about his son, John – later John the Baptist – and about Jesus (Luke 1:67–79). Simeon's announcement that Jesus is the salvation of Israel is also declared to be from the Holy Spirit (Luke 2:25–35). Matthew makes the connection even more strongly, by insisting that the baby in Mary's womb "is from the Holy Spirit" (Matthew 1:20).

This sets the pattern for Jesus's ministry; the Gospels make clear the early church's understanding that Jesus's work was undertaken in perfect concert with the Holy Spirit's activity. At Jesus's baptism, the Spirit takes centre stage, landing on Jesus in the form of a dove while a voice from heaven proclaims the unity between Father and Son (Matthew 3:13–16; Mark 1:9–11; Luke 3:21–22; John 1:29–34) and John the Baptist announces that Jesus will baptize with the Holy Spirit (Matthew 3:11; Mark 1:8; Luke 3:16; John 1:33). This is an intriguing combination of events, which tends to support the doctrine of the Trinity as it eventually developed. Here, we see Jesus's work attested to by the Father and blessed by the Holy Spirit. This is immediately followed by John the Baptist's public declaration that Jesus has the capacity to direct the work of the Holy Spirit in people's lives. This manifests a unity of understanding and action, combined with a distinction of persons, which is precisely what the doctrine of the Trinity intends to express.

The story of Jesus's ministry continues in just this sort of harmony with the Holy Spirit (and the Father, but we are discussing the Spirit). In Luke, Jesus is "full of the Holy Spirit" as he is "led by the Spirit" into the wilderness where he will be tempted (Luke 4:1). Jesus is "filled with the power of the Spirit" as he begins his ministry in Galilee (Luke 4:14), and announces that "the Spirit of the Lord" is upon him, as he announces his mission (Luke 4:18). Celebrating the successful work of people whom he has sent on mission work, Jesus rejoices "in the Holy Spirit," before reminding people of the unity between Father and Son (Luke 10:21).

Moreover (as we have noted previously), the author of Luke is very likely the same person who wrote Acts, which commences with one of the main works of the Holy Spirit in the Bible: Pentecost and the birth of the church (Acts 2:1–42). Jesus's ascension marks the conclusion of his earthly ministry. Then, in Luke's account, the community of Jesus's followers appoints a new disciple to take Judas's place, indicating a firm decision to continue as a group (Acts 1:12–26). Note that this is a sect of Jews who follow Jesus; there is not yet an independent "church," as we know it. On the Jewish feast of Pentecost (50 days after Passover), many of Jesus's followers assemble in Jerusalem, as Jesus had commanded. Suddenly, there comes the sound of a rushing wind. What seem to be tongues of fire appear, separate and land upon Jesus's followers. They are "filled with the Holy Spirit" and find themselves speaking about "God's deeds of power" in the languages of everyone present; since this is a special feast day, there is a great variety of people in Jerusalem, from all over the Ancient Near East.

To onlookers, this looks like the activity of drunkards. However, Peter speaks to the crowd on behalf of the group. He announces that the crucified and risen Jesus is the fulfilment of Israel's expectations, quoting Hebrew prophecies from Joel (Joel 2:28–32) and the Psalms (Psalm 16:11 and 110:1). Salvation and "the gift of the Holy Spirit" come through Jesus, for Jesus has "received from the Father the promise of the Holy Spirit" and "has poured out this that you both see and hear." Peter's preaching brings a massive response: the text speaks of 3000 baptisms that day.

The church traces its formal existence to this moment. At Pentecost, the church is constituted as the community of the Holy Spirit, preaching about Jesus the Christ and the Reign of God, and carrying forth the work of the Reign. The author of Acts makes this argument in his concluding assertion: "They devoted themselves to the apostles' teaching and fellowship, to the breaking of bread and the prayers." By the time that Acts was written, the main characteristics of church life are firmly in place; the author traces them to Pentecost. The Christian community is rooted in the activity of the Holy Spirit. The Spirit is the source of our response-in-love to God's generous gift of Godself, shown forth in Jesus the Christ.

And what of the rest of humanity? What of the rest of the created order? Is the response-in-love limited to those who are formally members of the Christian church? This question will be dealt with in greater detail in the section on salvation ("Can non-Christians be saved?"). The brief answer, however, is that anyone who responds to God by doing God's wishes is living in the power of the Holy Spirit. The activity of the Holy Spirit as founding and maintaining the church does not, in any way, prevent the Spirit from working in and through all of creation, including those who do not know about Christianity or have rejected it. Indeed, this is precisely the point with which our discussion of the Spirit began; the Spirit works through all of creation. In addition, Hebrews such as Bezalel did not know about Jesus. Moreover, we have no way of knowing how Bezalel would have reacted had he been around to meet Jesus. To insist that Christians own the Holy Spirit is neither reasonable nor biblical. As the Gospel of John reminds us, "The wind blows where it chooses, and you hear the sound of it, but you do not know where it comes from or where it goes. So it is with everyone who is born of the Spirit" (John 3:8). The Holy Spirit's work is directed by the Father, who is like the originating idea for all things. We can only look for evidence of the Spirit at work, in visible signs of God's Reign – whenever and wherever they occur.

Salvation

3

What is salvation?

Most of us have had the experience of being approached on the street by someone who asks the question, "Are you saved?" For many, this is an awkward experience. The average person often does not even understand the question; plus, the mode of delivery tends to be pretty intense. The decision must be made now, the interrogator seems to insist, and you must identify yourself as being "in" or "out," without knowing what is involved in the choice.

The language of being "saved" is only one of the Christian ways of describing what God does for us. It is, however, the most popular among certain groups of evangelical Protestants. For contemporary Westerners, therefore, it is a language that has very immediate relevance. It appears throughout the New Testament and is especially popular in the letters written by the Apostle Paul.

The first thing to be said about salvation is that we cannot save ourselves. This is just as true in theology as it is if we find ourselves drowning in the middle of a lake. Salvation is something that only God can provide. God's will is that it be for everyone. God is not creating and transforming the world for the benefit only of a few people, but for everyone and everything. As Paul indicates, "In Christ God was reconciling the world to himself, not counting their trespasses against them" (2 Corinthians 5:19). In the Letter to the Romans, he points out that "the creation itself will be set free from its bondage to decay and will obtain the freedom of the glory of God" (Romans 8:21).

The word "saved" implies that humanity and all creation are being kept from some undesirable fate and given something better. Christianity asserts that we are being saved from death. We need, however, to be clear about what "death" means. It is isolating ourselves from God – from the one who gives love, joy, peace, meaning, purpose, all of the things which justify life. There is true freedom in these things, as we shall see in a later discussion ("What is freedom?"). Evil flows out of this rejection of God and God's gifts; death wants to destroy things which give life to others. This is the bondage of death, from which God will save us.

There is a choice to be made. Often, however, we simply avoid the decision. We opt to put our heads down and take refuge in busyness, hoping that the difficult questions of life will pass us by. Unfortunately, this is much the same as choosing death; it sets us up for a slow slide into meaninglessness. One morning we wake up and suddenly find existence to be completely pointless. Or we simply choose death. Indeed, every time that we opt to do something destructive, we are choosing death. Either way, we wall ourselves off from God intellectually and spiritually (this is what "hell" is).

That is why the Second Letter to the Corinthians goes on to say,

"At an acceptable time I [God] have listened to you,
and on a day of salvation I have helped you."
See, now is the acceptable time; see, now is the day of salvation!" (2 Corinthians 6:2)

The decision of whether to choose life or death is always before us; in that sense, the call has an immediacy to it. At every moment of every day, we have the option of accepting God's way or rejecting it. God will always give us the gift of life, if we will accept it.

This immediacy is emphasized by the role into which Christians are placed by their baptism. Earlier, I quoted from 2 Corinthians 5:19, about God's reconciling work in the world. That verse concludes with the assertion that God is "entrusting the message of reconciliation to us." It is our task to tell the world of the joy to be found in living life in God and of the pain which is the inevitable consequence of refusal. We have the most wonderful work in the world: telling people about God's gift of eternal life.

What is God's grace?

"Grace" is a word in common usage, with a variety of meanings. However, Christians tend to employ it in a technical sense, which needs some explaining. The word "grace" means simply that God creates, redeems and sanctifies us as a gift. We cannot do any of these things on our own; nor can we force God to do them. Instead, our attitude in life must be one of thankful response to God. Such a response is, itself, a product of the work of the Holy Spirit within us. Thus, our gratitude, if it is real, will be accompanied by the participation in God's life that the Spirit always seeks to cultivate in people's lives. We will come to know and do the good (see "What is the good?"), the will of the Father, precisely because the Son transforms us and the Holy Spirit empowers us.

By grace, then, God enables us to fulfil the purposes of our lives. We are given the capacity to understand ourselves and the world to the degree necessary to do the particular work for which we have been made. Your work is not my work; through the Son, each of us has been formed in a specific way, to accomplish certain things in the Father's plan. Because our minds and senses are imperfectly attuned to the voice of the Holy Spirit, we do not always do that work as well as we might. Nonetheless, the Father continues to call to us, while the Spirit gives us strength to respond. Besides, God has a way of dealing with the consequences of our failures, as we shall see in our discussion of redemption ("What is redemption?").

Before we move on, though, we must address another aspect of God's gracious gift to us. As we attend to the voice of the Holy Spirit and answer through the Spirit's strength, we grow to know and love with God's knowing and loving. Of course, we cannot do these things as perfectly and completely as God does. However, we can come to understand and value God and our neighbour for who they are, rather than what they do for us.

Turning to God because of what God can do for me is really a fundamentally selfish attitude. Often, I suspect, it is not even a true turn to God; the cry "Save me!" can easily contain too much pride and avarice. The cry "Change me!" is more appropriately the

Christian response to God. If that is our attitude, then God will help us to find God and love God for who God is: the One who is most worthy of love. Moreover, God will help us to understand the world around us – its people, places and things – and to love them for what they are: divine creations and worthy of love. This is not a simplistic approach to life, dedicated to ignoring ugliness. Rather, this is God's way, knowing about all the mess and loving still. Living in God's love is participation in God's life; it is the eternal life which is God's free gift to us.

What is eternal life?

As Christians, and the Bible, often say, "God's gift is eternal life." At sports events in the United States, people often hold up signs saying "John 3:16." This activity strikes me as pointless, since the only ones who can understand the signs already know the Bible verse. Nonetheless, that particular verse is very important. It says that what God gives through Jesus the Christ, the Son of God, is eternal life. The following verse emphasizes that eternal life is salvation, and God intends it for the whole world.

What do you think of when somebody mentions eternal life? Most people focus on life after death. Often this idea comes with an associated picture from childhood, in which people sit on puffy, white clouds, wearing wings and playing harps. People tend to think of the word "eternal" as being the same as "everlasting." In theology, though, the two words mean very different things.

"Everlasting life" is long life. It may be something that came into being and will never stop existing. Or, it may be something which always was and always will be. Either way, something that is everlasting goes through time, step by step. Time is the succession of events; one thing happens after another. Everlasting means surviving through everything that happens, one thing after another.

As we have seen in our discussion of the meaning of "eternal" ("What do we mean when we speak of God as 'eternal'?") this is

not the way God is. God is in all things, all the time; God is present
with everything, at the same time. Time and space do not limit
God; we cannot get physically closer to God or further away from
God. Nor can a time be imagined in which God is not already
present. "Eternal" simply means that time and space do not impose
limits. Only God is really eternal, because all created things live in
time and space. However, we can share in God's life and know
something about what being eternal means. We can transcend
ordinary human limitations. We become "participants of the
divine nature" (2 Peter 1:4), because by "his divine power" Jesus
the Christ "has given us everything needed for life and godliness"
(2 Peter 1:3).

Eternal life is life with God, knowing God's love and sharing
God's work. As Jesus says in John's Gospel, "This is eternal life,
that they may know you, the only true God, and Jesus Christ
whom you have sent" (John 17:3). This is a gift that God gives to
anyone who responds to God by doing what God wants. It is the
life of the Reign of God, the gift that we receive through Jesus the
Christ, as we have seen. Christ's Incarnation, life, death, resurrection and ascension make eternal life possible, by uniting us and
all of creation with the Father.

Christ also shows and tells us the meaning of eternal life.
Choosing life means that we commit ourselves to undertaking the
work which God gives us. Being absolutely true to the mission
which God has given me, even if I must suffer for it, is my basic
task for God's Reign. We see Christ's sinlessness precisely in his
wholehearted and unflinching commitment. Even as Jesus faces the
ultimate pain of a brutally imposed death, he tells the Father that he
would prefer not to undergo the pain, but that he would submit to
the Father's will (Matthew 26:39; Mark 14:36; Luke 22:42).
Whatever I am made to do, which suits my talents and capacities
and serves the good (see: "What is the good?"), defines my mission
and goal in life. Following Jesus means fulfilling that mission,
seeking that goal, to the end. I must seek to do my work as well as
I am able to do it.

As Dorothy L. Sayers has pointed out, this is how we live the life
of the Trinity (Sayers, *The Mind of the Maker*). In our work, we
conceive ideas, formulate them and respond to them. We also give

these ideas form, by making things. As a consequence of our activity of making, we cause the world to respond. If we are living eternal life, then we will create in love. We cannot always assume that the world will respond in love – that is the primary lesson of the crucifixion. However, each of us can continue in faithfulness to the mission which God has given us. Therein, we find our own resurrection and ascension.

We have also seen that life in the Reign of God implies a fundamental commitment to social justice. Our work must, somehow, further God's peace and justice in the world. We must help people to know and participate in God's work in creation. At the heart of eternal life is the biblical command to love God and love neighbour; indeed, we are even called to love our enemies and the people who hate us (Matthew 5:44; Luke 6:27, 35). Living in love enables us to live God's life, for love is the divine characteristic that we see in God's activity of creating and transforming us. This is the creative life for us. In it, we participate in the world's resurrection and ascension.

This opens us to God's gift of joy in the present, because each of us can know fulfilment. Whatever is ours to do, God will enable us to do. God will give us life and pleasure in our tasks – this is the lesson of the resurrection and ascension.

Unfortunately, this joy is inevitably partial, alloyed by pain and suffering. Every encounter with the Reign of God seems also to be a meeting with something that will hurt somebody. We live in a world full of wars and rumours of wars, where even the task of growing up cannot be accomplished without some hardship and destruction. This is because our taste of eternal life in the present is merely a foretaste of a completion to which we look forward (theologians call this a "proleptic" experience – from the Greek *proleptikos*, which means "anticipating"). We see, in this looking forward, the meaning of Christian hope: we trust that God will complete the work of reconciling all of creation to Godself. Then we will know eternal life in all its fullness. Meanwhile, we enjoy the gift of life in the "here and now," a gift that is available to all who will open their hearts in love to God and the world.

Opening our hearts in love is the response to God's activity that the Holy Spirit brings about. The Son's work makes eternal life possible by creating the unity between divine and human which draws us into the life of God. The Son makes us children of God. The Holy Spirit accomplishes the transformation in us that enables us to live as God's family, doing what God would have us do. This distinction is most easily explained through the use of the traditional theological terms, "justification" and "sanctification."

What are justification and sanctification?

Justification and sanctification are aspects of eternal life; they are things that God does for us while enabling us to become the best "us" that we can be. The terms are theologically loaded, because the debates about them have been intense and acrimonious. However, both justification and sanctification are visible occurrences in Christian life, which means that some basic understanding of them and their theological roots is fairly simple to reach.

"The gift of God is eternal life," as we have already seen ("What is eternal life?"). The Father wants us to be reconciled with God. For us, reconciliation includes coming to understand who we are and what we can be. There is much that we do not know, about God, ourselves, and the world. In contrast, the Father understands everything, fully knowing both Godself and the created order. For us, the possibility of true joy and fulfilment in life depends upon entering into the loving relationship with God which makes true knowledge possible.

"Justification" describes the process of being set right with someone. The term has forensic overtones: it literally means "to be made just." God invites us to live in right relationship with God, ourselves and all the rest of creation. As a matter of fact, though, we do not always do so. Sometimes, we deliberately do what we know to be wrong; at other times, we fail to do what we know we ought to do (which comes to the same thing, in the end). Both of these sorts of actions have an alienating effect. Such actions create a sort of spiritual, psychological and intellectual distance between what we are and what we ought to be. We also find ourselves distanced from God. Our relationship with God is broken. Our lives and the life of the world are broken. We have acted unjustly.

Justification is the process of being made right again. At its root is the single event of the birth, life, death, resurrection and ascension of Jesus the Christ. Jesus the Christ unites humanity with divinity, transforming the humanity and preparing it for life with God. Jesus absorbs the worst evil which we can do and demonstrates that God can take it, overcome it and transform it into good. Jesus shows us that resurrection and ascension are ultimate, as we shall see in our discussion of the doctrine of redemption. All of this activity sets the created order right and announces that it has been set right. The Reign of God is here.

However, the Holy Spirit encourages us to recognize that the glorious vision of God's Reign is not always evident in our own behaviour. We still behave unjustly, failing to live in love with the Father and meet the Father's standards. Thus, we must continually return to this moment of justification and make it our own. We cannot simply accept, on one occasion, that Jesus the Christ has reconciled us to God and move on from there. Through the power of the Holy Spirit, which enables us to respond to God's call to us, we can and must reappropriate this action of justification on a regular basis. For those who live in a sacramental church context, this is the function of the sacrament of reconciliation (commonly known as "confession"). Others accomplish the same thing through routines of prayer. In either case, we need to be genuinely sorry for the evil done and the pain caused; this is generally known as "contrition." We must do what we can to make things right, ameliorating the evil consequences of our actions and seeking to make new, good things happen; this is "penitence." In order to be able to move forward in life, growing in God, we must know that we are forgiven and reconciled; this is "absolution."

The point, then, is that justification is accomplished once, for the life of the world, in Jesus the Christ. However, this is an eternal action; its effects touch all of time and space, so it is always present for us to enter into. Moreover, we need to enter into it, often and routinely, because we are always in need of justification. It is a gift once given, which ought to be enjoyed often.

Having said all that, we know that life with someone whose sole, or even primary, intention is to remind us that we sin would be nothing but depressing – a "serious downer," in today's lingo. Would you marry someone who did nothing but remind you that you mess up? If not, then why would you associate with such a God? The tendency on the part of some Christians to harp on the problem of sin, to the exclusion of all else, is one reason why many people never find the joy of life with God.

God's work with us is not simply about responding to the evil that we do. God did not create us in order to have the opportunity of forgiving us. Creation and Incarnation are about something much richer and more exciting: God is sharing God's life with us. That is what "sanctification," which means "being made holy," is all about. The Father's purpose for us is that we should live and work in concert with God and, thereby, fulfil the meaning of being human by being more than human The Son became human for this. In the birth of Jesus the Christ, humanity and divinity meet and humanity is elevated into true holiness. In the life of Jesus the Christ, we see what holiness means. In the death, resurrection and ascension of Jesus the Christ, we are shown the victory of holiness – a victory in which we can share.

The primary work of the Holy Spirit within us, then, is precisely to foster the unity between us and God. Our participation in the divine nature, which we spoke about in the context of "eternal life," is the essence of sanctification. The deepest riches of Christian life are to be found as we come to know God more deeply and, thereby, come to know ourselves more profoundly and accurately. The consequence of the Holy Spirit's sanctifying action within us is the growth of virtue and right action. We find ourselves better able to know what is good and more inclined to do it. That is why the Apostle Paul says, "the fruit of the Spirit is love, joy, peace, patience, kindness, generosity, faithfulness, gentleness, and self-control" (Galatians 5:22–23). The Holy Spirit enables us to love more as God loves, transcending the human limitations of self-interest and immediate concern. As we do so, we grow in the highest virtues with which God has endowed us. Far from being a "downer," this is the most exciting and joyful thing that can happen to us. This is why the gospel is truly "good news."

Both justification and sanctification begin to affect us at very young ages. In a limited but very real way, sanctification takes hold as soon as we are able to learn. Everything that we learn about loving and doing the good, when internalized and lived, contributes to our ability to live God's life. The form which our life-in-relation-to-God will take varies according to our capacity for love and for intellectual development, as well as our historical context.

Sanctification is a process of growth, in which the Holy Spirit is always actively encouraging us to respond in love. We are called to continual conversion, more-and-more becoming the people whom God wishes us to be. Thus, ongoing sanctification, the continuation of growth, is partly dependent upon our willingness to respond. We are always free to reject God's call. We may choose a life of habitual destructive actions, which cause us to become less than human rather than accepting God's gift of something greater. The time in which to respond to the Spirit's prompting is always now. Yesterday's acceptance of God's gift is helpful only in that it sets the stage for today's.

Being a Christian can offer some advantage in this process. Knowing what God is doing in the world and our lives can help us to respond eagerly. We have an especially great opportunity to participate in God's redeeming work in the world. As with all knowledge, however, Christian knowledge comes with added responsibility, because God expects us to live up to what we are taught. We who know that God is love are particularly called to share the gift of God's love with the world.

Our justification has already been worked for us. However, we take hold of it and participate in it every time that we recognize an evil which we have done, are truly sorry and commit ourselves to making amends. As soon as we are old enough to have some form of moral awareness, we know the Holy Spirit at work in us, aiding us to do that which is good and respond appropriately when we fail to do so. Our knowledge of this work is inevitably partial. God approaches us according to our talents and capacities, seeking our fulfilment within the limited horizon set by our particular human identities. God does not ask us to do what we cannot, but we are always responsible for what we can know and do.

Moreover, we are blessed by the Spirit when we act according to the Spirit's leading. There is a kind of comfort and joy that comes with doing the right thing. It is felt to an even greater degree when we find it in mended relationships with God, our neighbour, and the whole created order. Christians can know this blessing in an especially powerful way, for we hear God's absolution proclaimed. We know that we are forgiven when we apologize sincerely and seek to bring good out of the evil which we have done. We know that, through the work of Jesus the Christ, we and all of creation are forgiven and God is acting to mend all relationships.

Justification and sanctification, then, are works that accord with the Father's will, brought about through the birth, life, death, resurrection and ascension of Jesus the Christ, and enacted in our lives by the Holy Spirit. These two processes are parts of the one whole which is eternal life – the great, divine gift to us.

What is redemption?

"Redemption" is another word which Christians use to describe what God has done for us. The Apostle Paul says that "Christ Jesus ... became for us wisdom from God, and righteousness and sanctification and redemption" (1 Corinthians 1:30). "Redemption" is a term rather like "salvation"; where "salvation" implies that we are being saved from something, "redemption" implies that we are being redeemed from – and for – something. It sounds like a grocery story coupon in use; the store redeems the coupon, accepting it in exchange for an article that the shopper wishes to own. Redemption is something that Christ accomplishes for us, especially (though not solely) through his death and resurrection. Our redemption is accomplished in us and all of creation by the Holy Spirit, causing new life in places where destruction has had its impact.

God's redemption is something that everyone has observed. Because of the work of Jesus the Christ and the Holy Spirit, redemption is built into the nature of creation. Visiting the ruins of a very old building, such as a church, temple, or monastery, can provide a clue to how the process operates. We don't have that many old ruins in North America, but they can be found in many other parts of the world. Often such places have a beauty which comes from both the original structure and nature's activity in reclaiming the space. The building is no longer a building – perhaps it lacks a roof and parts of the walls – but it has a new meaning and power as a ruin. Strange as it may seem, this is God's redemption in action.

Every time something is destroyed, God brings a new creation out of the destruction. This is true as part of the biology, chemistry and physics of the universe. It is also true on the personal level. Every trouble that we go through can be used by the Spirit to make us richer, stronger people, able to do new and different things. We grow by facing difficulties. This is where we learn lessons which make us able to confront the next set of complexities to come our way. This is redemption: out of potentially or actually destructive circumstances, God brings something greater than had existed before.

This is not cause for easy optimism, however. Sometimes we are trapped in a cycle of destruction, where everything bad seems to lead to something worse. This may be our own fault; we can easily take a momentary setback and allow it to dominate our lives. The computer misbehaves and suddenly I'm angry at everybody! It can simply be the situation, though. People lose their jobs and cannot find another, then fall into poverty and depression. Life becomes hellish.

Even at these times, though, God is acting to redeem. Moreover, we are given the chance to participate. Our job is to work at bringing creation out of destruction, helping everyone to know God's redemption. We can help the poor, the needy, the unemployed. We can bring creation in other ways, too. Orchardists and vineyarders show us new life every spring, with the joy of the blossoming trees and growing vines. When grapes are taken off the vines, the grapes die; their death gives us beautiful wines which enrich our lives. Thus, our basic tasks of work help us to know God's redemption.

In a play by Dorothy L. Sayers, an architect discovers redemption. He describes a time when a worker ruined a statue of a saint, so the architect rebuked the worker for carelessness. However, the architect then saw a new vision of what the stone might be and made it into a hippogriff (an imaginary animal).[1] This is how God works with us. Evil is not undone, but it does not win. Instead, God makes something new.

Thus, we see God performing the "taking away" which is redemption, purchasing good out of evil. The death and resurrection of Jesus the Christ demonstrate how God does this. Indeed, Christ's death and resurrection may even be the root cause of the principle of redemption in creation – certainly, Paul thinks so. The complicated intermingling of creation and redemption often makes distinguishing the two rather difficult. The distinction is an artificial one anyway. Both are activities occurring through the work of the Son of God; they are eternal in cause and their effects are felt throughout time, so that we humans can never really say where one begins and the other ends. Is God creating when God uses Desmond Tutu's "Truth and Reconciliation Commission" to help forge a new sense of the possibility of racial harmony in South Africa? Yes. Is God redeeming when God uses this commission to show the world a healthier way to respond to the evil of racial discrimination and repression? Most certainly.

In Christ's death and resurrection, then, we see God's principle of redemption at work. It is God's assurance that destruction is not, and will not be, ultimate. God's power is always greater than the power of destructive forces. Humanity may draw into action all of its might, seeking to put God to death. Out of this effort, God brings life. No matter what evil we commit, God is still present, acting redemptively. This is what God does for each one of us, if we permit it. The Holy Spirit will work with us, redeeming us from evil and making us into the children of God.

When we become Christians, we make a formal commitment to participate in the work of redemption. That is life in God's family, joining in divine activity. To those who do not share that

---

1. Dorothy L. Sayers, *The Zeal of Thy House* (New York: Harcourt, Brace and Co., 1937), 100.

commitment, it often looks like a form of bondage. It looks that way because it is a form of bondage, limiting our choices. It is, however, precisely the kind of limitation that God lives, the limitation which is built into God's nature. God chooses only the best possible course of action. That binds God, but it is divine freedom. Redemption brings freedom.

What is freedom?

Christians say that God gives them liberty. Indeed, one of Martin Luther's most famous writings is called "The Freedom of a Christian." However, non-Christians are often puzzled by this, because to them a Christian life looks anything but free.

There are two common reasons for this puzzlement.

The first is that Christians sometimes mistake Christianity for respectability. We equate "sin" with "anything of which society disapproves." As a result, we become uptight and grim; we look as if we never have any fun. People do not want to become involved with a church whose only purpose is to be as rule-bound and boring as possible. Jesus, of course, was anything but respectable, and his first recorded miracle was to change water into wine for people who had already imbibed rather freely at a wedding reception.

The second cause of difficulty is that we tend to misunderstand the meaning of freedom. To us, the word "freedom" usually means "the ability to do what we want to do." This is a false definition; it defeats itself. Often, what we want to do would destroy our ability to choose and act. Some people, given this kind of freedom, would opt to sit in front of the television, eating and drinking, for hours. People who do this for a while will not be much good for anything else. If they do it for too long, they will not be able to get out of bed. Their deaths will be hastened. Their choice will have destroyed their ability to fulfil their greatest desire. What appears to be freedom has led them into slavery and destruction.

Freedom is better understood as "the capacity to know and do the good." People who choose the good option (in this case, healthy diet and an appropriate level of exercise) often find that the world magically opens up to them. Many more good things become possible for these people. Their joy in life increases. They discover the beauty of God's creation. They come to love life, which can help them to know and love the Giver of Life. This is true freedom, for it leads to joy and meaning. It is the work of the Holy Spirit, giver of true life.

Freedom is to be found in fidelity to the purposes for which God has made us. Sometimes, that binds us to a hard road. The Spirit may call us to do difficult things, say hard words or live in demanding circumstances. Moreover, the results are not always as beautiful as those in the scenario of which I have just spoken. For Jesus, exercising true freedom meant going to a nasty beating and excruciating, public execution. However, from that action of faithfulness to the divine will came the transformation of the entire *cosmos* and the joy that Christians down the ages have known. That brutal death was a step toward the resurrection which changed everything. True joy is to be found here, also, though it is tinged with sorrow at humanity's destructive actions. The example of Christ's death suggests that freedom is redemptive; it takes us (and others, as well) out of bondage.

The free choice, then, is always the choice of the greater good, for it benefits us and all of creation. Working in us, employing all of our talents and capacities, the Holy Spirit will enable us to grow in the ability to recognize greater and lesser good. One of the complications of human life is that the world does not usually present itself in terms of evidently good and obviously evil options. Instead, we tend to be faced with situations in which all of the options will enable some sort of freedom and some degree of bondage. Our task is always to choose the greatest freedom possible for the whole cosmos, even if that involves suffering and destruction for ourselves; this is what Jesus the Christ did. Ultimately, in his bondage – imposed by his task and by the authorities – is his and the world's freedom.

Freedom, therefore, is not a simple thing. It certainly is not the same as licence, which is mere childish wilfulness. Instead, freedom is life in God's love, knowing God's redemptive work in history and participating in it. Freedom is the life of heaven.

What is heaven?

"Our Father in heaven;" When we all get to heaven;" "Will you be in heaven?" Some Christians talk about heaven a lot, though, interestingly, Jesus did not speak about it very much; he usually talked about the kingdom, or Reign, of God – which is why our focus has been on the kingdom.

Heaven is a complicated word, because it seems to talk about a place. As we most commonly think about it, heaven takes up space. We tend to think of it as being occupied by God and a bunch of white, winged and ethereal beings which we call "angels." Some people would want to add humans (who have left this world) to the picture, while others believe that people become angels upon arrival in heaven.

There are, however, many difficulties with this picture. The first is that God does not take up space: God is eternal, which means that God is present, at once, everywhere and at all times. That means that there is no place which is not God's home. Moreover, Christian theology has usually insisted that, whatever angels might be, they do not take up any space, either.

To quote a friend: "How many angels can dance on the head of a pin? As many as want to!"

Heaven is where we find God, which can be anywhere. God is everywhere and we cannot get physically closer to God by dying. Instead, we meet God when we are loved and when we love. Then we get a taste of God's presence, which is a taste of heaven. You can know heaven in relationships with family and friends; in giving to those in need; in doing your work; in camping, hiking, canoeing and being with the world which God has given us; or in a myriad of other contexts.

What about life after death? Christians believe in everlasting life, which means that we insist that God continues to be present with us after we die. However, we do not know what that looks like. We know only that we are under the care of the God who loves us, now and forever. Living in that care is living in heaven, with God.

What is the kingdom of God?

Jesus talked constantly about the kingdom of God (or the kingdom of heaven, which is Matthew's phrase for the same thing). The kingdom is at the centre of the Lord's Prayer, which is Jesus's answer to his followers when they asked him how they should pray.

> Our Father in heaven,
> hallowed be your name.
> Your kingdom come,
> your will be done,
> on earth as it is in heaven.
> Give us today our daily bread.
> And forgive us our debts,
> as we also have forgiven our debtors.
> And do not bring us to the time of trial,
> But rescue us from evil.
> (Matthew 6:9–13; see also Luke 11:2–4)

There are many things about this prayer which are worth discussing, but now we will focus on what it says about the "kingdom" or "Reign" of God. The Greek word is *basileia*. It refers to the area over which a ruler's power extends. The Reign of God is present wherever God's power is shown forth.

The phrase "your will be done, on earth as it is in heaven" begins an explanation of what the kingdom is. Heaven is wherever God lives, which is everywhere – we have only to see it and choose to participate in it and enjoy it. To do this, we need to do God's will, because that is what shows that we are aware of God's

Reign and that we claim citizenship in it. The kingdom is present whenever and wherever what God wants done, is done.

The mere existence of creation, then, is the most obvious instance of God's Reign. The created order comes into being through God's Word. Moreover, God's life-giving work through the Holy Spirit is evident throughout the universe. God's will can be seen in this; God reigns over everything.

Human life, though, is more complex than the life of an asteroid. We are not merely redeemed; we may participate intelligently and voluntarily in redemption. We always face the possibility of choosing a kind of freedom which is not available to a piece of rock hurtling through space. We can share in God's Reign, by living God's creative life. For us, doing God's will means choosing the greater good, even if we must suffer for it. Moreover, we recognize that we may need to face pain in the process. The Apostle Paul describes the whole of creation as "groaning in labour pains;" he adds that we "groan inwardly" as we await the "redemption of our bodies" (Romans 8:22–23). We do not seek out pain. Instead, we ask that God will free us from it and from the clutches of evil. Nonetheless, we know that facing such challenges is part of living for God's Reign.

More is implied by the phrase "Your kingdom come" than a simple willingness to do God's will. This language is an expression of Christian hope, of looking forward to the completion of God's Reign, when God's will shall be done by all people and things, everywhere. To the Christian eye, the presence of God's Reign in the here-and-now is evident; we are surrounded by love, joy, peace and beauty. To that same eye, works of destruction, which militate against God's Reign, are also evident; we are surrounded by war, strife, poverty and loneliness. Calling in prayer for the coming of the kingdom means asking God to do what God has promised, fulfilling God's work in our lives and in our world.

Theologians speak of God's Reign as being both now and not yet. As a consequence of the Triune God's creating and redeeming work, the Reign of God is a feature of creation's life from the beginning. The Son has united divinity and creation, while the Spirit enables the created order to respond appropriately. Nonetheless, the Reign also has a "not yet," future, dimension. We look forward to a time when the Father's will shall be done everywhere and by all things.

Thus, we call out to God while making our own loving commitment to God's work – a commitment which begins with our own willingness to forgive others, including those responsible for the evils which impinge upon our own lives. We call out to God in faith, trusting that God will accept us and continue God's work in us, beginning with an act of forgiveness toward us for the evils which we do. We call out to God in hope, knowing that God will do as God has promised – redeeming the whole of creation and enabling it to serve its true purpose.

The mundane plants itself right in the middle of this cosmic vision and the devout soul-searching which accompanies it: "Give us this day our daily bread." As we have seen ("How does Jesus's life serve the Reign of God?"), Jesus's values might be other-worldly but his work is attuned to the specific needs of the people around him. He feeds the hungry, showing the mathematics of the Reign of God whereby a small portion of bread and fish can feed thousands until they are satisfied – and leftovers are then gathered. He provides drink for the thirsty, showing the joy of the Reign of God by taking water and turning it into the finest wine. He heals the blind, the lame and the suffering, showing that physical distress will be banished under God's Reign. He shares God's peace and justice, showing the love of God to a woman whom the authorities wished to stone for being caught in adultery. He raises the dead and himself overcomes death, showing that neither physical nor spiritual death will have a place in God's Reign. Clearly, Jesus the Christ did not become incarnate to deliver us from the physical world, but to redeem it.

On the basis of what we have seen in the "Lord's Prayer," we can point to the Reign of God as the situation in which God's will is done. It has both present and future dimensions, and the created order is part of both. We are called to live in the Reign of God, proclaim it and act upon it, while looking forward to its completion.

Much more than this, we cannot say. Final details are in the mind of the Father. If it is true that no conversation about the Reign of God is complete without some mention of Jesus's parables, it is equally true that the parables do not take our investigation much further than it has gone already. They tend to provide hints and warnings, rather than concrete details.

The parable of the wise and foolish bridesmaids (Matthew 25:1–13) indicates that we must always be watching for God's Reign, for we cannot know its coming before it appears. The sower (Matthew 13:1–23; Mark 4:1–9, 13–20; Luke 8:4–15) and the talents (Matthew 25:14–30; Luke 19:11–27) emphasize the importance of our attentive response to God's call, while the yeast (Matthew 13:33; Luke 13:20–21) tells us that God can take the work of the few and use it to transform the whole world. The treasure hidden in the field and the pearl (Matthew 13:44–45) show the value of God's Reign; we should dedicate our lives to searching for it.

The mustard seed (Matthew 13:31–32; Mark 4:30–32; Luke 13:18–19) reminds us that God's Reign often comes through small actions undertaken by the powerless, while the labourers in the vineyard (Matthew 20:1–16) and the prodigal son (Luke 15:11–32) suggest that the joy of God's Reign is equally available to all people and is not dependent on the extent of their work. The lost sheep (Matthew 18:10–14; Luke 15:1–7), the two sons (Matthew 21:28–32), the great dinner (Matthew 22:1–14; Luke 14:15–24), and the pharisee and tax collector (Luke 18:9–14) show that God does not forget the weak and those without status, who are often greater in God's eyes than the mightiest of the world's authorities. The lost coin (Luke 15:8–10) and the unjust judge (Luke 18:1–8) remind us that God reaches out to all who will recognize their need for transformation, while the weeds and wheat (Matthew 13:24–30, 36–43) and the net thrown into the sea (Matthew 13:47–50) declare that evil has no place in God's Reign.

The overall focus of the parables seems to be upon the Reign of God as an instance of God's generosity. We have the opportunity – indeed, we face the urgent demand – to be aware of God's gift and respond to it, but the Reign is God's to provide. And God gives it to all who desire it, without regard to stature or capacity, at the time of God's own choosing. Throughout all of the parables runs a sense of the great value of the Reign of God; it is the ultimate vision of all that is truly good. Thus, we return to our starting point, because the ultimate vision of the good is the will of the

Father. Our task is to seek that will and strive to do it, in the power of the Spirit, while looking forward to the day when all things shall be ordered as the Father intends.

What do we mean when we talk about "Christ's return"?

This is a term which refers to the final completion of the Reign of God. Biblical prophecies tend to be attached to the conversation about God's Reign, as, for example, in Luke 21:20–36. This passage announces great troubles to come and, in the midst of it all, the return of the Son of Man "coming in a cloud with power and glory." Thus, when people see all of these difficulties, they will know that "the kingdom of God is near."

In some ways, this vision can be a real challenge to the contemporary believer. The picture of a man swooping down in a mass of water vapour droplets, in order to set the world to rights, seems too much like the script for a B movie. We find it difficult to take seriously, in part because of the awkward physicality involved; bodies do not behave like that and it all seems rather unnecessary, anyway.

In fact, the Christian is not required to accept any particular picture of the fulfilment of the Reign of God. The belief that God will set the world in order, establishing God's reign of justice, is a central tenet of Christianity. It is the meaning of Christian hope. How people picture that happening is a matter on which we may legitimately differ. Belief that God will complete the world's purpose is a decisive commitment but acceptance of any precise understanding of the way in which it will occur is not. We need only conform to the vision of the Reign of God given to us by Jesus the Christ, with its priority of love for God and neighbour.

I realize, however, that some will be intrigued by the prophecies of Jesus's return. This may be especially true of those who are familiar with the fundamentalist insistence upon belief in a bodily return, which precisely conforms to the above picture of Christ on a cloud. For those people, I include a more careful discussion of some of the relevant issues.

> As they were watching, he was lifted up, and a cloud took him out of their sight. While he was going and they were gazing up toward heaven, suddenly two men in white robes stood by them. They said, "Men of Galilee, why do you stand looking up toward heaven? This Jesus, who has been taken up from you into heaven, will come in the same way as you saw him go into heaven. (Acts 1:9–11)

The promise that Jesus will return is a portion of the ascension story which we have not previously discussed. It is, if anything, more difficult to understand and accept than the picture of Jesus rising up into the sky and vanishing. The Gospel of Matthew concludes with Jesus saying, "And remember, I am with you always, to the end of the age" (28:20), which seems much easier to understand. Yet the idea that Jesus has left and will come back appears in scattered references throughout the New Testament. Indeed, Matthew records Jesus as promising to return very soon.

> For the Son of Man is to come with his angels in the glory of his Father, and then he will repay everyone for what has been done. Truly I tell you, there are some standing here who will not taste death before they see the Son of Man coming in his kingdom. (Matthew 16:27)

This is a vivid prophecy, with notably more precision than the brief section which we have taken from Acts. Some explanation is definitely called for.

On the face of it, the most obvious explanation is the simplest: Jesus plans a bodily return to earth. This is the position taken by Charles Erdman in *The Fundamentals*, which is the set of essays which gave the name "fundamentalism" to a modern movement in Christianity.[2] Such an argument appears to do justice to the text;

---

2. Charles Erdman, "The Coming of Christ," in *The Fundamentals: A Testimony to the Truth*, Vol. XI (Chicago: Testimony Publishing, 1910) 87–99.

Salvation

it displays the kind of blunt, physicalist, "literalism" which is a hallmark of fundamentalist interpretation of the Bible. The Enlightenment's preoccupation with empirically measurable "facts" is evident in Erdman's interpretation.

This is only true up to a point, however. Note that the text is quite explicit in its assertion that some of those present would not "taste death" before Jesus's return. Erdman is forced to change his tack when he comes to the problem of an "imminent" return. It cannot be intended as "immediate," since it has not happened. Erdman notes correctly that the biblical discussion reflects the expectations of the early church and insists that the biblical references to the immediacy of Jesus's return suggest only that the timing cannot be known to us. Therefore, the early church, like today's church, must always be ready. This is fair comment and it certainly does justice to Jesus's assertion that "about that day and hour no one knows, neither the angels of heaven, nor the Son, but only the Father" (Matthew 24:36). Matthew's portrayal of Jesus's prophecy in chapter 16 is much more explicit, though. There, Jesus says that some of those present will not die before he comes, implying that he has a reasonably clear idea of when it will happen. There is a conflict here, which cannot be resolved by merely overlooking the definite prophecy. Erdman seems to have taken the approach of "literalism if necessary, but not necessarily literalism."

Let us begin, then, with this problem of timing. Is Jesus simply wrong? The thought is not unthinkable. Undoubtedly, Jesus was limited by the thought-world of his time. If we could enter his life and ask him to explain day and night, we would surely get an unsophisticated explanation which we would recognize as being incorrect. His divine nature revealed to his humanity only what was necessary in order that the mission be completed. However, this question of his return seems to touch his mission rather closely; surely he would have been correct in whatever he said about it. Then again, wrong which time? Is he wrong, on the one hand, to declare that he does not know or, on the other, to suggest that he knows, but have his prophecy remain unfulfilled?

The difficulty seems to be that the early church was not altogether clear what Jesus had said or what the church was expected to believe about this matter. We have seen an ambiguity in Matthew's Gospel. The argument comes into the open at the conclusion of John's Gospel, which evidently reflects a debate within the community. The text has Peter asking about the future of the "beloved disciple" (who is anonymous in John's Gospel, but is traditionally regarded as being John, the disciple).

> When Peter saw him, he said to Jesus, "Lord, what about him?" Jesus said to him, "If it is my will that he remain until I come, what is that to you? Follow me!" So the rumour spread in the community that this disciple would not die. Yet Jesus did not say to him that he would not die, but, "If it is my will that he remain until I come, what is that to you?" (John 21:22–23)

The community in which John's Gospel was formed seems to have been caught in a debate. The question is whether the "disciple whom Jesus loved" (who is identified as the author of the Gospel in 21:24) will live to see Jesus's return. Some members of the community said that he would, but the text's author is doubtful. He is not clear when the end will come. Instead, he emphasizes the conditional "if" in Jesus's statements. The whole passage seems to encourage the reader to return to the decisive clarity of 21:19 and Jesus's ringing command, "Follow me." Fidelity to Jesus the Christ should be our focus, rather than silly quarrels over the time when the Reign of God will be fulfilled.

If we turn from the issue of timing and attend to the specific mechanics of the event, then a number of difficulties face us immediately. The post-resurrection appearances of Jesus tend to suggest that Jesus's bodily presence is so constituted that it could appear in the sky and descend to earth, to rule here. In other words, it could happen and people are free to believe that it will.

On the other hand, this tends to make the Reign of God into something narrow and local, when the whole tenor of the biblical and historical development has been to make it larger and more universal. As it stands, God's Reign is manifest everywhere in the world. If its completion is in a simple, physical, manifestation of Jesus, then God's Reign takes on the nature of an earthly kingdom. It must be ruled by power, from a particular location – Jerusalem is the place usually named, because of its symbolic resonance as the biblical centre of the worship of God. Theologically, this vision of a Reign of God that looks like any other empire is not merely unhelpful – it is all wrong.

Moreover, the physicalist vision of the "end times," along with a kind of literalist reading of various symbolism-laden biblical prophecies, has led to an unhealthy meddling in Middle Eastern politics. The American "Religious Right," especially, has developed a fascination with the fulfilment of fundamentalist-Christian expectations in Palestine. This preoccupation adds a powerful and influential variable into the Arab-Israeli disputes, which are already fraught with ancient tensions.

Fundamentalist-literalist readings of the prophecies of Jesus's return are not really tenable on the grounds of careful Bible reading. They are also theologically and politically unhelpful. We are much wiser to allow the language of Christ's "second coming" to stand as a symbolic term, describing the fulfilment of the Reign of God and the central place of Jesus the Christ in its establishment. Then we can follow the example of the Gospel of John and turn our eyes to Jesus the Christ, who says, "Follow me."

Can non-Christians be saved?

This is a question which sparks a lot of debate within Christian theology. Different people will give you different answers. These tend to fall into one of three categories: exclusivism, inclusivism, or pluralism. The position that I have been working with throughout this book is an inclusivist one.

Exclusivism insists that only Christians can know who God is. This position insists that Jesus's statement, "I am the way, the truth and the life. No one comes to the Father except through me" (John 14:7) means that anyone who does not explicitly stand within Christianity is rejected by God.

Inclusivism says that God is Trinity, as Christians believe, and saves people through the transforming action which we are able to see in Jesus the Christ because of the work of the Holy Spirit within us. Inclusivists do not, however, believe that people need to be formally Christian in order to know God. Anyone who responds to the world in love is responding in the power of the Holy Spirit and is being saved. The inclusivist position is a response to the reality that many people have never heard of Jesus, while others have heard of him and rejected him because of flaws in the people who convey the message.

Pluralism asserts that all major religions are true and right ways to reach God. Each religion functions within its own thought-world and is valid on its own terms. Anyone who follows a major religion faithfully is doing as God asks. This position is a response to our world in which many religious views co-exist; deciding whether one is more true than another seems impossible to many people. These people value belief and commitment and want to avoid religious conflict, which can flare into violence.

Few people are really pure exclusivists; most people understand that some room must be made for those who have never heard of Jesus or have no way of judging Christian claims. Even the Apostle Paul, who is commonly regarded as an exclusivist, was hardly an unequivocal one. A commonly quoted passage is Romans 10:9, which says, "If you confess with your lips that Jesus is Lord and believe in your heart that God raised him from the dead, you will be saved." This verse states the positive, "If you do these things and mean them, then you will be saved." It does not state the negative, "If you do not do these things, then you will not be saved." Indeed, Paul does not seem to intend the negative, given that large portions of the argument before and after the quoted section are dedicated to talking about the salvation of Israel; this includes a lengthy dissertation on the faith of Abraham and how God "reckoned it to Abraham as righteousness" (Romans 4, esp. v. 9). Abraham, of course, never talked about Jesus the Christ, since Abraham died long before Jesus was born. There is also an important – though often overlooked – passage early in Romans, which suggests that Paul is more open than we tend to think.

For he (God) will repay according to each one's deeds: to those who by patiently doing good seek for glory and honor and immortality, he will give eternal life; while for those who are self-seeking and who obey not the truth but wickedness, there will be wrath and fury. There will be anguish and distress for everyone who does evil, the Jew first and also the Greek, but glory and honor and peace for everyone who does good, the Jew first and also the Greek. For God shows no partiality. (Romans 2:6–11)

The focus, here, is on people's actions, as indicating their response to God in faith. Jews or Greeks who have never heard of Jesus appear to be on the same footing as explicitly Christian people. This is more in accord with the cosmic vision of the Incarnation which we have seen in the gospel story, than with a strict exclusivism. Biblically and theologically, exclusivism does not seem to be supportable. In spite of these difficulties, and a variety of clashes with Christian thought, exclusivism is still taught in many places.

Pluralism, on the other hand, makes no sense. Aside from the difficulty of establishing what a "major religion" is, pluralists face the problem of trying to explain how opposing views can be true. The problem arises when we compare Christianity with Buddhism, for example. Christianity is firmly committed to the existence of a God who lives, creates, loves, becomes incarnate, dies and is resurrected. Buddhism is equally committed to the assertion that no such God exists. Existence is not a modifiable predicate; in other words, either a thing is or is not. This is precisely what we mean when we say, "You cannot be half-pregnant." Assertions that both statements ("The Triune God is" and "The Triune God is not") are true can be sustained only by compromising the word "true," so that it does not say anything about existence but only comments on what one thinks – "You think a statement is true, so it is true for you even if it bears no relation to reality." In other contexts, this is what we mean by insanity.

Alternatively, pluralism can be sustained by ignoring aspects of different religions and pretending that they are really all alike. Christianity and Buddhism, then, are reduced to manifestations of the common search for meaning. This is, certainly, an aspect of both Christianity and Buddhism. However, there is much more to both of these belief systems and the remainder is hardly irrelevant.

To treat them in this way displays the greatest disrespect to both viewpoints and, especially, to the great teachers from both traditions.

Most Christians are inclusivists of some kind. That means that they believe Christianity's claims to be true; God is creating and transforming the world as the major creeds of the Christian church assert. However, inclusivists do not believe that people must be formally Christians to respond to God and do God's work in the world.

Some Christians say this simply because there are many people in the world who have never heard of Christianity and the belief that God will not have anything to do with them as a result makes no sense. There are many others whose encounter with Christianity is badly distorted by the messenger, whether because the one who is passing on the news does it poorly or because that person's life undermines the message. Surely, God continues to work in the lives of those who meet such false messengers.

The inclusivist position has deeper roots than these, however. Christians believe that anyone who shows love is showing God's love, for all love comes from God. When we see people doing loving actions, displaying care for other people and all of creation, then we know that the Holy Spirit is at work. That is true even when those who show love entirely deny the presence of God. I believe that this is the message of Jesus the Christ and it is the heart of what I have been trying to convey in this book.

In addition to the above considerations, we recognize that there is something true and helpful in the words that most people have to speak. If anybody is truly wrong about absolutely everything, then that person will inevitably die – spiritually and physically. Short of that extreme is everyone else, all of whom (Christians included) are right about some things and wrong about others. Christians have become painfully aware of our history of imposing our views while ignoring the insights which other people have. We know that the God who loves us is transforming the world in love. But we are coming to realize that we do not always know when, where or how. Thus, we need to stand firm in our message, while humbly waiting, watching and listening for the Reign of God – wherever it is found.

What happens to people who reject God?

As the Apostle Paul notes, "The wages of sin is death" (Romans 6:23). Rejecting God's call brings about a kind of spiritual, intellectual and psychological separation from God. For as long as we exist, in whatever form, we cannot be physically separate from God; all things have their life from God, who is present in and to all things which possess any kind of existence. However, we can wall off our consciousness, so that we block any awareness of God and God's call to us. We can do this either intentionally, by specifically choosing to oppose the good in any decision of which we are aware, or unintentionally, by merely sleep-walking through life and avoiding any clear choice of direction.

The consequence of either path is a kind of cycle of decline in what we might call our "souls." Pride grows, hand in hand with dishonesty. We become angry with the world and envious of others, as the world fails to serve us in the way that we expect. The soul becomes numbed to the call of God – displaying the blankness that has traditionally been called sloth. Avarice, gluttony and lust come to rule our physical being, as we are trained into habitual evil choice. Physical death is hastened, because of a failure to curb such destructive habits. The alienation from God that results from falling into sin is what we call "hell," the misery of attempting to exist without attention to God, in whom is the true purpose of our lives.

Of course, "all have sinned and fall short of the glory of God" (Romans 3:23). One or more of the above sins is likely to manifest itself in everybody's lives. This is why Jesus warns us of the dangers inherent in judging the state of another's soul. "Let anyone among you who is without sin be the first to throw a stone at her" were Jesus's words to the authorities who were gathered to execute a woman caught in adultery (John 8:7). Judgements must be made, for the sake of communal life, but there is no more dangerous task. All too often, we judge out of our own sinful desires, rather than out of a divine commitment to redemption. We need to be careful to ensure that we judge the life and actions of others only when necessary and that such judgements, when they must be made, are made in love of God and the other.

Approaching the sins of others in a sinful and censorious way, rather than the way of love, is the hallmark of far too much supposedly "Christian" comment. We do not know how God will choose to heal any of us, whether in this life or after it. The endless books and sermons that speculatively detail suffering and pain awaiting people who do not convert, right now, show too many signs of an effort to force others to do our will and join our group. Often, they are themselves sinful, giving evidence of a kind of spiritual pride that blinds us to God's work in others and leads us into great acts of destruction.

We know that sin is destructive, both of self and of other. We know, also, that God permits the sinful choice. We may reject God's overtures, committing ourselves to destruction. On the other hand, we know that God is "reconciling *the world*" to Godself, through Jesus the Christ, and "not counting their trespasses against them" (2 Corinthians 5:19). We know that the Holy Spirit is everywhere present, transforming hearts and minds. We know that the ways of the Spirit are God's ways; even if we cultivate in ourselves an awareness of divine activity, God's means of reconciliation are often mysterious and opaque to us.

We cannot say, with any assurance, that God will leave anyone in an ultimate state of alienation from God. The theology of God's Reign suggests otherwise. In the words of the Apostle Paul: "As I live, says the Lord, every knee shall bow to me, and every tongue shall give praise to God" (Romans 14:11). These words are based in a prophecy of the Reign of God found in the second part of Isaiah (45:23). Built into the Christian – and the Jewish – hope is an expectation that all people will respond appropriately to God's love eventually, whether before physical death overtakes them or afterward. God is working God's perfection in each of us, at the pace that God knows to be suitable to the character which God has given us. My task is to ensure that I can say with Paul, "It is no longer I who live, but it is Christ who lives in me" (Galatians 2:20), so that I can share life with God, other people, and the whole of creation.

We do not know precisely what will happen to any of us after death. Perhaps people like me, who still display great imperfections, will find that the process of growth and transformation will continue. The idea of the life after death as having an element of continuing purification is the impulse behind the medieval doctrine of purgatory. Such an impulse is both reasonable and an acceptable part of a Christian theology. The decadent aspects of purgatory – such as the sale of indulgences (a kind of "Get out of purgatory free" card, that one could buy for oneself or someone else) – are merely disgusting. Moreover, the tendency to identify distinct places where one goes after dying (heaven, purgatory, hell, for example) is dangerous. Our physical deaths do not have any impact on God. God can reach us under any circumstances. We have no reason to believe that our physical deaths will render us inaccessible to God's love. More likely, God continues to approach us then as God reaches out to us now, with the offer of eternal life.

What, then, of biblical statements that seem to imply a permanence of destiny for each of us, as a consequence of divine judgement? There is something uncompromising about the story of the sheep and the goats, related in Matthew 25:31–46. Matthew's Gospel leads up to this sermon with parables, two of which conclude with evildoers being placed "where there will be weeping and gnashing of teeth" (24:51; 25:30). Neither of these stories, however, suggests anything about the duration of this pain, the description of which is an accurate representation of life in attempted isolation from God. The sheep and the goats story ends with the goats, who have not fed the hungry and clothed the naked, being driven into "eternal punishment" and the sheep, who have shown God's generosity, entering into "eternal life." Matthew uses the word "eternal" to speak about life in the Reign of God. In Matthew 18:3–13, people who care for children find the "kingdom of heaven," while those who cause children to stumble find the pain of eternal fire. In Matthew 19:6–21, the rich young ruler may find eternal life by selling all of his possessions and giving to the poor. In all of these cases, eternal life is the life given by God, which is life in communion with God. Eternal punishment is separation from the eternal God, but not necessarily permanent. God routinely saves people from out of such misery.

Luke's Gospel contains the example that people seem most commonly to turn to, when they want to defend a doctrine of permanent punishment. Here we find the story of Lazarus, a beggar, and the rich man at whose gate Lazarus called for alms (16:19–31). Lazarus and the rich man die. In the place of the dead, the rich man suffers. Seeking alleviation of his pain, he calls to Abraham, whom he sees "far away," and asks that Lazarus be sent to bring him a taste of water. In the story, then, the evildoers have the ability to communicate with the righteous. The rich man's request, though, displays all of his old arrogance; in his eyes, Lazarus remains no more than a servant, at the disposal of the truly important. Consequently, Abraham reminds the rich man of the benefits which he received in life and points out that there is "a great chasm . . . fixed" between them, which Lazarus cannot cross.

There is a boundary here, but whence comes the boundary and what maintains it? The rich man has erected a wall of sin around himself. Treating Lazarus as his slave is not an indication that he is willing to allow the wall to be broken. The consequences of sin, so far in the story, have led only to self-pity. The next step, then, is for the rich man to begin to show some concern for others. He does so, asking that Lazarus be sent to the rich man's family, to warn them that their sin will lead to suffering. This is merely a small shift, from focusing on his own pain to being concerned about that awaiting his brothers. Nonetheless, it displays real spiritual growth. Thus, the story implies that even after death, God's transformation occurs in the lives of those who have done evil – a category which, in the final analysis, includes all of us. Rather than emphasizing the permanence of human rejection of God and of consequent punishment, this text seems to be built around a kind of purgatory. The sense of the text is that the rich man is at the very early stages of growth in divine love, with the wall of his resistance to God starting to break down. Incidentally, Abraham will not send Lazarus to preach to the brothers, either, announcing that Moses and the prophets should be adequate and that the resurrection of a man from the dead would not likely change the hearts and minds of people who ignore God's words.

This narrative may not be intended as a story of what happens after death. Very likely, it is a cautionary tale about the need to care for the hungry. Indeed, it begins with a fairy-tale sort of opening: "There was a rich man who was dressed in purple and fine linen." The story is also a reminder that even the resurrection of Jesus the

Christ will not convince everyone to respond to God's call, which is Abraham's concluding point. It ends unsatisfactorily, though; one wishes that more had been said about the rich man's development and Abraham's responses. This might give us a clearer sense of the theological points which the author of Luke wishes to make with the story. Nonetheless, the basic principle which appears to be at work is that God's justice is restorative – more precisely, transformative – aiming at the growth in Christ's life of persons and all of creation, rather than retributive, which is an "eye for an eye" exacting of payment. "God did not send the Son into the world to condemn the world, but in order that the world might be saved through him" (John 3:17).

Certainly, evil brings physical and spiritual suffering and death and we must warn people of this fact. Self-imposed isolation from God is truly painful and destructive. In all circumstances, though, we must stand with Jesus the Christ, announcing the good news of God's eternal salvation – a gift that is always available. The task of making this announcement is at the heart of the Christian community, so we will now turn to discussing the church, its life and its meaning.

The Church

4

What is the church?

To the contemporary ear, talking about "the church" sounds odd. After all, what the average person encounters is not one, single, ecclesiastical entity, but an endless variety of churches. Commonly, different denominations will establish buildings directly across the street from each other. No efforts toward working together can overcome the sense of competition which that symbolism annnounces.

In the context of a multiplicity of churches, the language of "mere Christianity" rings hollow. Denominations differ profoundly. There exist small, exclusive churches, dedicated to individual salvation and purity, that do not permit others even to know when their communion services occur. Such groups are not telling the world the same thing as large, open, churches that focus on social justice and may allow people of any faith or no faith to participate in their eucharistic services. Treating both of these as branches of Protestant Christianity is historically and theologically accurate, but hardly enlightening for Jane or John Brown, walking down the street.

How, then, can we speak of "the church"? This sheer multiplicity is, believe it or not, a good starting point for our investigation. One of the things that the variety of denominations points to is the human and historical dimension of church. When we become Christians, we always do so in a historical context, in response to a particular message conveyed, in a specific place and time. Different denominations reflect different ways of being Christian, which often have their origins in responses to historical circumstances.

The contextual dimension of churches is both a strength and a weakness. They are institutions and such organizations tend to retain the marks of their founding and development. Lutheranism, for example, carries forward the suspicion of "works righteousness" and the joyful emphasis upon salvation as God's gracious gift, received in faith, both of which are part of the 16th-century response to abuses of Christianity. Along with a dedication to historic Christianity, these emphases are sustained by an institutional commitment to a certain way of reading the Bible. A number of "Confessions", dating back to the early years of Lutheranism, serve as constant reminders of the message which Lutherans are called to share with the world.

As Lutherans respond to contemporary circumstances, they are able to turn to a rich heritage of belief and action, combined with a history of ongoing reflection upon matters of belief and action. This can enable a kind of counter-cultural attitude, in which Lutherans are freed from the limitations of current trends of thought by a longer view. Moreover, the Lutheran heritage has been feeding institutions (hospitals, universities, seminaries, ecclesiastical structures) for centuries; consequently, Lutherans have large church structures in place to support a variety of ministries that might not otherwise be possible. On the other hand, the very permanence of their heritage can create a kind of immobility, limiting openness to new trends of thought or forms of ministry. Large structures with long histories are creatures of momentum; turning them usually requires great quantities of time and energy.

In contrast, small churches of recent founding can often move very quickly, responding to contemporary styles, needs and concerns. However, they may not have the institutional strength of older churches and may need to rely heavily on the charismatic leadership of one or two people. They may also tend to be captured by contemporary trends in thought, because they lack some of the heritage needed to inform them of the limitations of the current viewpoint. A balancing act is possible here. Older and younger, larger and smaller, different denominations all have something to offer Christianity. They can serve God in a variety of ways and sustain a variety of understandings of the Christian message. Different groups can engage in mutual criticism, which can be very healthy (although it can also be quite destructive).

I suspect that you have noticed a rhetorical shift in our

conversation. We have gone from speaking of "the church" to discussing "churches." How do we get back to "the church"? Are all churches part of the one church? There are different opinions about the relationship among individual denominations. The Roman Catholic Church, which includes a majority of the world's Christians, says that the only true church is the one in full communion with the Pope, Bishop of Rome; all other churches are somehow deficient. Other denominations take other approaches. Commonly, Christians recognize one another by three signs: (1) use of the Bible as the ultimate standard for Christian belief, in company with (2) the ecumenical creeds (Apostles' Creed, Nicene Creed), established by the Early Church (*see commentre 'Church' above!*), and (3) performance of baptism and eucharist, which are the basic rites of Christian communal life. The church is, by and large, composed of groups of people who display these three signs, although a very few consider themselves Christians and even participate in the World Council of Churches – an organization in which Christians meet to discuss matters of belief and action – without committing to one or more of the common practices.

Christians share some other things, enabling us to recognize similarities even in the context of profound difference. Participation in educational activities might well deserve first place on our list. The church, however understood, is always an educational institution. It is a place where people teach and learn about God. The world is often dominated by human fear and self-interest. We are always in need of a place where God is the central actor in the conversation, providing us with an opportunity to re-think the meaning of our lives. There we learn about God's work in the world and the significance that it has for us.

Of course, the church is not simply a classroom. We do not participate in it merely to discuss ideas about God, interesting as such talk might be. Instead, the church is a place of transformation, a context in which God changes lives – our lives. Many, though not all, of us prepare ourselves to allow God's work in us and God changes us into the people that he made us to be.

The church, therefore, is a sacrament, an outward and visible sign of God's gracious action. Sacraments always have two aspects: (1) a part of creation, and (2) God working in and through that part. The people who enter into the church's life are the essential piece of creation with whom, and through whom, God is working in the sacrament of the church. One of the most helpful characteristics of this way of seeing the church is that sacraments assume flaws. The created order is a necessary part of a sacrament and anything which is created has limitations and shortcomings. The church is an imperfect, but real, sign of God's working, because Christians make a commitment to respond (in the power of the Holy Spirit) to the transformation which God offers the whole world. We are changed and being changed. As the popular slogan has it: "Please be patient. God isn't finished with me yet." I am not attempting to excuse the church's flaws. Christians have, if anything, less excuse than others for destructive actions – some of which have been truly monstrous. Instead, I am suggesting that a sacrament consists in God's taking something which is imperfect and slowly, carefully, transforming it into what God would have it be.

The church, then, is always on a journey toward the Reign of God (see "What is the kingdom of God?"). Consistent with our name – the word "*ekklesia*," Greek for "church," means "a group of people called together" – we are called to participate in God's Reign and make it known to others. We do this in the context of worshipping God, as we listen to God and re-commit ourselves to relationship with God. When we assemble together, we are reminded of the greatness of God the Creator, and the wonderful gifts of life and work that God gives us. In worship, we give thanks to God for these gifts. The worship context is also an important act of community-building, as we share together in life with God. Being in right relationship with God demands right relationship with our neighbours.

Our worship life, then, ought to lead inexorably to a life of service to God's Reign. We must commit ourselves to knowing and doing the good, while paying special attention to the needy of the world. The church fails in its task when it is not an instrument of God's work to and for all people. Love and faithfulness toward God always lead to active love toward the neighbour, so that we must be a servant church. We face a priority of doing over speaking, of showing forth the Reign of God in our actions of service.

Nonetheless, we also have the vital task of sharing the good news of God's transformative work in the world. Our trust that God is bringing God's Reign in the present and will complete it in the future is the knowledge and hope that we offer to a world beset by hopelessness. The church is called to be a herald, someone who hears good news and tells other people about it. Part of the job of people in the church is to look for God at work. This means paying careful attention to the whole world, in its tiniest and largest aspects. When we see good things happening, then we must call people's attention to the good things that God is doing. We are announcers of good news!

Knowing God to be present and at work in the world and in us, we show ourselves and others something of who God is. We have the joy of living God's life, eternal life; if we allow this to happen to us, then we see the world change around us. To do all of these things, we form organizations, the denominations which we discussed earlier. The structures of the church help us to learn, worship, share, serve, grow, and be transformed. We try to maintain these common goals, even as we differ in our beliefs about how they may best be accomplished in any particular time and place. Because we are human, our approaches will always be partial and inadequate; therefore, we serve as correctives to each other, reminding one another of forgotten or ignored aspects of the good news. Thus, in the messy way that humans have, a bewildering variety of people and their denominations make up one church, with a common root in the salvific work of the Triune God and a common mission to live out the meaning of that salvation.

Why go to church?

We have spoken about "the church" and particular denominations as instances of "church." Now we are discussing a third use of the word "church," which refers to public meetings organized by each denomination. Ordinarily, these will occur on Sunday mornings, in recognition that Jesus rose on the first day of the week and Pentecost also occurred on that day, though other times may be set aside, also. A meeting will usually have a set agenda, with time for worship and prayer. Usually, a sermon will be included; a sermon is a sort of speech, in which a person discusses some aspect of God's work in the world, often as a reflection on a reading from the Bible. This is called "preaching." Meetings of the kind that we are discussing tend to occur under the leadership of trained and appointed ministers; some of the tasks involved, such as leading the rites and preaching, call for a high degree of expertise. Many other people participate, however, because such meetings are at the core of Christian life. The most commonly recognized mark of Christianity is the practice of going to church.

There have been times in Western history, such as the 1950s, when church attendance has been the norm for most of society. People just did it, whether out of genuine commitment or for less praiseworthy reasons. This is not one of those times. Now, people are more likely to find Sunday to be a good time to catch up on the rest which they could not get on other days, or to travel or to take the children to various activities. These are worthwhile ways to use time. Why do differently? Why go to church? What does the practice accomplish?

Life can often seem to be meaningless. We get caught up in the tasks that we must do or the things that we can buy; then we stop and ask "Why?" and realize that we do not know. In church, we talk about the purpose of life and enter into the activities which make life meaningful. Church is, in part, educational; we meet to talk about who God is and what God is doing. We hear about other people's encounters with God throughout history; this helps us to know God. In other words, at the centre of church life is a conversation about God's Reign. Developing a deeper under-standing about God and God's work enables us to know ourselves and our world better. There is psychological and spiritual strength in having a sense of meaning. Moreover, identifying goals and strategies in life becomes much easier when we have some understanding of what life is all about.

Intentionally spending time with God can be life-changing – for the better. Worshipping God helps us to know our place in the world, to be aware of ourselves and our needs. It provides a chance to speak to God about our own needs and the world's needs. It also gives us the opportunity to be silent in the presence of God, allowing God to form us as people who can hear God throughout the daily round of life. Thus, we enter into God's life in the world. In church, we can have a real sense of the Holy Spirit taking hold of us, calling us, transforming us and giving us the joy of life in God.

Why join the church?

Joining the church can be a bit different from going to church. We tend to think about going to church as giving us something. Often the question, "Why should I go to church?" is rather similar to "What's in it for me?" Joining the church, though, has more to do with what we can give to God and other people. The joy which we receive from it is that joy which comes from giving a valuable and worthwhile gift to another whom we love. This sharing of gifts creates a bond which remains even through adversity and strife. Sometimes we fight with one another, but we are God's people and God does not let us go.

When we identify ourselves as part of the church, we are saying that we participate in the church's life. We are stating that we have a commitment to it. That means giving. We give ourselves to God and the world. Of course, we will benefit. Nobody can tolerate a situation that is all give and no take for too long. However, one of the conditions of receiving is often that one pledges oneself to generosity. This is one of the great paradoxes of life.

Giving ourselves means, first of all, that we commit to being with God. Nobody can really get away from God, who is present in and to everything. However, forgetting about God is all too easy. As part of the church, we make a point of listening to God, as well as speaking to God about our needs and those of the world. Recognition of the activity of the Holy Spirit within us is precisely what makes church, *church*. Christian community is always a response-in-love to divine transformation in history; the Spirit generates that response in us. Careful attentiveness allows us to know God at work, to hear God's call, and to identify our own opportunities for ministry.

We commit to helping those in need while praying for them. The church has always taken a lead in providing food, shelter, clothing and medical care for those who cannot afford it – and even for those who can, since many of today's hospitals were founded by churches. "Blessed are you who are poor, for yours is the kingdom of God" (Luke 6:20) is a watchword for the church's life. In Matthew 25, the distinction between the sheep and the goats – those who participate in God's work and those who do not – is that God's people feed the hungry and give water to the thirsty. Jesus the Christ lives in those who give. Matthew's more surprising point, though, is that Christ is in those who receive. Christ the King, ruler in the Reign of God, announces to the faithful: "Truly I tell you, just as you did it to one of the least of these who are members of my family, you did it to me" (v. 40). This is an instance of the great divine exchange, where those who are in Christ serve those in whom Christ is. Here, we see the Holy Spirit at work, showing forth God's loving presence.

Commonly, people who shun the church when they are comfortable turn to it for help immediately when they are in need. That is one of the reasons that the church exists. We are called to show the light of Christ to the world, even when people do not want that light. Then, we are called to serve when those same people have need.

Thus, we also provide help for people who have intellectual, emotional and spiritual needs. People who need to understand the world and their place in it come to us. People who feel lost or scared often find the church to be a welcome home. "Blessed are the poor in spirit, for theirs is the kingdom of heaven" (Matthew 5:3), is another of the church's guiding principles. Living the life of Christ helps us to know something of the Father's meanings and the Father's peace. We can serve the Reign of God by sharing those meanings, and the peace which they bring, with people who are aware of their spiritual poverty. Of course, our more intellectual activities, such as teaching and preaching, can help such people. Pastoral visits and other such personal attentions can be beneficial. Often, though, entering into the church's worship and discovering the presence of God is the decisive transformative factor in the lives. We may demonstrate the wisdom and love of Christ all day and all night, but only the activity of the Holy Spirit within can enable the needy to receive and accept the gifts which the Father wants them to have.

Matthew's emphasis upon poverty of spirit is very helpful for contemporary Westerners, who tend to be among the world's wealthiest, if wealth is measured in possessions. One of the church's central tasks is to remind people that the purpose of work is not to enable the accumulation of material stuff. Through Christ, each of us is made with particular talents and inclinations, in order that we can do specific things well. The Father's purpose for all of us is that we perform our work in a way that shows forth the Reign of God. In other words, our daily work, whether it be serving as lawyer, homemaker, labourer, swimming instructor or CEO, is divine work. We ought to do it to the glory of God, at the prompting of the Holy Spirit. The church, therefore, must support people in their non-ecclesiastical activities and it does so, though not as much or as often as it ought. Worship and prayer life contribute to forming us for our tasks. Many of the church's educational activities (for example: study groups or days; Christian schools, colleges and universities; Christian books and magazines) can be helpful, also.

The church provides leadership in society in the activities about which we have spoken, as part of our share in Christ's ruling activity. We seek to understand what our society ought to be doing and share our conclusions with others, by advocacy, teaching (churches founded many of our universities and schools and continue to lead some of them), political involvement and other means. Some people are uncomfortable with the church – as church, rather than merely as individuals who might belong to churches – participating in the public realm like this. In *A Letter Concerning Toleration,* John Stuart Mill argued that politics has to do with present life, while religion has solely to do with what happens after we die (Indianapolis: Hackett, 1983. Originally published: London, 1689). On those grounds, he insisted that religion should be completely walled-off from the public sphere. Mill was fundamentally wrong about both politics and religion. Politics deals with matters of ultimate value; in an afterlife, what we do for society here-and-now is going to be important. Similarly, religions are rarely – perhaps, never – solely concerned with life after death. At the core of Christianity is a set of expectations about how we will live in community now. Consequently, the church simply must display leadership in public society. Failing to do so would compromise the church's witness entirely.

Joining the church means entering into the great exchange, in which we receive gifts from God to be shared with God and others. In return, we give ourselves to God. For many, this is the greatest call imaginable. Moreover, it is essentially a communal call, rather than a purely individual one. Thus, most people do not go to church in order to be alone (though there are always exceptions). The church is often called "the body of Christ," a phrase which comes from the writings of the Apostle Paul. The language of "body" is important in this context. It carries the sense of incorporation into the life and work of Christ that we can experience in the church and which is a consequence of the Incarnation (see "What is the significance of Jesus's birth?"). We are bound together with Christ and with one another, brought into one body by the Holy Spirit. Even the messy, flawed life of the church, characterized by disunity as much as unity, offers the benefit of common life. God's call to love and care for one another and the world always stands before us and the Spirit is always at work within us.

The focus upon being a body also emphasizes the sacramental aspect of what we do; we are a visible, physical, fully human manifestation of God's creative and redemptive work. We have the opportunity to show the Holy Spirit in action, to ourselves and the world. Moreover, as Paul emphasizes (I Corinthians 12:4–20), my talents and tasks are not the same as those of every other person. In the Christian community, as in the larger community, there are a variety of gifts and a variety of things that need to be done. No-one can serve God in all of the ways that I have outlined, even to a minimally helpful level.

Consequently, the church is always in need of new members,

who are often drawn by the opportunity to serve. Commonly, people go to church in order to receive and stay to give. They have discovered the wisdom in Christ's saying, "It is more blessed to give than to receive" (Acts 20:35). By the curious mathematics of the Reign of God, those who give themselves to God and their neighbour fulfil the mission which God gives them, so long as they do so in accordance with the talents and purposes for which God creates them. As a consequence, such people find themselves to be truly blessed and fulfilled – and the mission of the Holy Spirit is completed in them.

Worship and Prayer

5

Why do we pray?

In the Epistle of James (5:16), there is a verse which says: "The prayer of the righteous is powerful and effective. Elijah was a human being like us, and he prayed fervently that it might not rain, and for three years and six months it did not rain on the earth. Then he prayed again, and the heaven gave rain and the earth yielded its harvest."

It all sounds pretty simple and straightforward. Pray constantly and with real faith and determination, then whatever you ask will happen. Pray for the sick; they get well. Pray for dry weather; the clouds vanish. Pray for rain; you'd better get out your coat. Obvious, isn't it?

Only, it doesn't really happen that way. We pray for the sick and sometimes they do get well. Then again, sometimes they die. We pray for dry weather and sometimes it dries up. Then again, sometimes the flood waters rise. We pray for rain and sometimes it rains. Then again, sometimes prolonged drought is the apparent outcome. I lived in Saskatchewan for five years, long enough to become accustomed to plagues of Old Testament proportions – it's always too dry or too wet, or there are too many grasshoppers. Is the problem simply that the people in Saskatchewan do not pray enough? Or, do they not go about it in the right way? But then, how much is enough? What is the right way?

In other words: How can we compel God and the world to do what we think is right? That is the real issue. We want the universe to follow our wishes. We want to be what we think God is.

We tend to think that God is something like an all-powerful traffic policeman, routing the world's events this way and that way. This person goes here. That person goes there. This thing goes here. That thing goes there. We want to be like that, too, ordering the world according to our own wishes.

Fortunately for us, that is not God's approach. God is definitely not the traffic-policeman. God makes us people with the capacity to build and tear down. To grow and reap. We can change the world through our decisions and actions. If we can do that, then evidently God has given us freedom. God invites us to work with God, rather than forcing us to do precisely what God would have us do. Indeed, creation would be pointless, if it simply functioned like a dolls's house, with God rearranging the furniture and dolls at will.

Why, then, should we assume that we should be able to run the world in this way, with God and creation at our beck and call?

Besides, that would be a recipe for disaster. I like to think of myself as a good judge of people and situations. In my more honest moments, though, I shudder at the idea of having the power to rearrange the world to suit my liking. The number of messes that I manage to create in any given day is already enough to test the patience of my best friends. Only imagine the consequences if I could force the whole world to do whatever I want! Everyone I know would run for cover.

Push that picture further. Imagine if everyone had that power, including those whom you most dislike or distrust. We'd probably stalemate each other much of the time, as we all pushed God to do things that are mutually contradictory. I would order up a nice, sunny day for a picnic, while a farmer is begging for rain. When God does find the opportunity to do something, it would be likely to be pretty messy, given the ideas that we humans are prone to cook up. Simply trying to picture us being able to run the world by getting whatever we want from God is impossibly ugly.

The irrationality of our idea that we can control God and the world with prayer appears to leave us with two questions: (1) Is the Epistle of James simply wrong about prayer? and (2) Why do we pray?

Is this passage wrong? I'm not convinced that it is, because I don't believe that it means the sort of thing that we've been talking about. The sort of healing to which James refers is not simple physical healing. James focuses on the connection between prayer and the forgiveness of sins.

> The prayer of faith will save the sick, and the Lord will raise them up; and anyone who has committed sins will be forgiven. Therefore, confess your sins to one another, so that you may be healed. (James 5:16)

And:

> My brothers and sisters, if anyone among you wanders from the truth and is brought back by another, you should know that whoever brings back a sinner will save the sinner's soul from death and will cover a multitude of sins. (James 5:19–20)

The illness to which this passage refers is not physical illness. The death is not physical death. Physical illness and physical death can be awful things. However, they are not the worst things that can happen to us. Spiritual illness is the worst illness. Spiritual death is the real death. Many people suffer it, even as they walk around, apparently healthy. This is the death that comes from rejecting God, choosing instead to live for destruction. People who exist in this death can be identified by the nasty, destructive things that they say and do. Such people have a crushing effect on the world around them.

When we do evil things, mistreating our world, our neighbours, ourselves, then we need to confess. If we do not, then we will face the consequences which are built into the world. Every time that we do something which causes harm, we are harmed. We become shaped as people who do harmful things. Life loses its joy and peace. First, we turn away from the destruction which we have caused, perhaps by refusing to associate with someone whom we have hurt or by avoiding a place where we have left some mess. If the wound is allowed to fester, then we find ourselves backing away from the whole community. We are left with ourselves – and we find no peace there. Indeed, if we allow the evil to grow in us, then we learn to hate ourselves. This is the spiritual illness, that leads to spiritual death.

The only answer to this is to admit that we have sinned against God, our neighbours and ourselves. We must apologize – to God, our neighbours and ourselves. We must seek spiritual healing and regeneration.

This, then, is one of the primary reasons that we pray. Prayer is an opportunity to reflect upon our lives, considering our thoughts, judgements and actions. In prayer, we can examine ourselves, taking a clear look at our meanings and motives. We can share these things with God. Where necessary, we can make apology to God and ourselves, thereby preparing ourselves to make appropriate apology and restitution to anyone whom we have wronged.

There is an age-old practice known as "confession," or, in the contemporary mode, "the sacrament of reconciliation." In this practice, we share our confessions with another person, as suggested in the reading from James. This practice is less common in the church than it once was. It is, however, an integral part of the twelve-step movements which help many people today. Do not overlook the therapeutic value of sharing one's needs and weaknesses with another person. There is something deeply cleansing about that act. Moreover, it can cause the other person to engage in prayer for us, which is always helpful.

This brings us to the question of what prayer does. The basic function of prayer is to align us with God and God's work in the world. Prayer does not change God; it changes us. Thanking God; praising God; apologizing to God; asking God's strength in certain of our activities – these are all ways of opening ourselves to God's presence within us. Committing ourselves to prayer means allowing the Holy Spirit to make us more like Christ, the image of God's self. The goal of prayer is that we might become sacraments, not wilful and destructive tyrants.

The same is true of praying for other people and all of creation. We open ourselves to their concerns and, thus, become instruments of salvation for others. Simply being reminded of those needs changes us and focuses us upon God's work in the life of the world. Also, prayer helps us to find ways to participate in God's work, the Reign of God. We become aware of what we can do to help the world see God's love.

This is what the text means when it speaks of bringing a sinner back from wandering. Praying puts us in a place where we can show God's love to those who need it. And, when it comes right down to it, that means everyone.

What is a sacrament?

Most Christians focus their life together around rites that we call "sacraments," though some Protestant churches reject them and the idea of them. A sacrament is a visible sign, something that we can see, which shows us something that God is doing. Moreover, that visible thing is being used by God to perform divine work. A sacrament, therefore, is an effective sign; it both shows God at work and accomplishes God's work, with the Holy Spirit operating in and through it.

In the most general sense, this means that everything is sacramental. The creation is an important sacrament because it helps us to see God at work everywhere; God is using the created order to fulfil God's purpose. Everything that God makes (which is everything that there is, with the exception of Godself) is employed by God for good and, therefore, shows some aspect of God.

There is a problem here, though. A sacrament accomplishes its work if we are made somehow more like God through it. That change in us is God's work. However, we can choose to participate in God's work in us or we can reject it, fighting God all the way. Moreover, sometimes people who love God and want to participate in God's work have a hard time seeing God in the world. Poverty, war, environmental abuse and other tragedies sometimes make God's love seem distant.

God is not distant or uncaring. Instead, God is always present in and to us and the world. However, we need to be trained to recognize God at work. Just as training is necessary for us to understand complex and beautiful music, so we need formation to know what God does in the world and how. The world may be intrinsically sacramental, a powerful statement by God about who

God is, but if we cannot hear and respond to that statement then the world is not sacrament for us. Even without knowing about sacraments, we derive benefit from them. The ancients did not need to know what we know about air in order for them to be able to breathe. However, being aware of God's sacramental working and understanding something about it enables us to respond and participate in it more fully. The Holy Spirit gladly and freely gives us the power to respond properly to God in love. However, the Spirit does not override our will and capacities; instead it works with them. Consequently, we need training in knowing God at work in the world, in knowing the Spirit's call and responding to it.

The church's sacramental life provides that training; it is a major part of what sacraments, in the more limited and common sense of rites of the church, do. Baptism brings people into the church; this is a celebration in which water is poured on the person receiving the sacrament. In baptism, we see cleansing and new life being given to the recipient. Eucharist (or Mass, or Holy Communion, or The Lord's Supper – it has many names) is a ceremony in which we share bread and wine (or grape juice). In the eucharist, we celebrate all that God does for us and we enter into God's life and work, committing ourselves to do what God wants.

Being baptized and joining in the eucharist are activities that help us to know who God is and what God wants for creation. The symbols speak to us; water, bread and wine can carry exceedingly vivid meanings. The words which are spoken as we employ the symbols are powerful. Plus, the elements (water, bread, wine, etc.) themselves are means by which God works in us; they are vehicles of God's power.

Consequently, sacraments have a transformative influence. They do not merely show us what God does. Instead, the fundamental power of sacraments is the change that they work in us and the world around us. Participation in them makes us into part of the Body of Christ, cultivating the divine life in us. Sacraments make us more like Christ and more completely citizens of God's Reign; this is especially true if we are willing to co-operate with the work of the Holy Spirit in us and the world. Sacramental life, therefore, is a decisive part of God's sanctifying work (see "What are justification and sanctification?"). As we live that life, we are changed; we become more able to know and do the good. Thus, we become instruments of God's transformation for the whole of creation. A single sacramental activity has a ripple effect, with boundaries that we cannot know. Moreover, we have a taste of what God's Reign is like when we participate in sacraments.

Baptism and eucharist are the church's central sacramental actions, though not the only ones. As we have noted, any action which manifests God's presence while working divine transformation in someone or something is a sacramental action, but churches also explicitly identify some activities as "sacraments" in a narrow sense. Formal sacraments are rites which can be traced to the work of Jesus the Christ: either he explicitly commanded that we do these things or showed by example that these are ways that God works.

All churches which talk about sacraments include the two that we have mentioned. These are sometimes called "Sacraments of the Gospel" because of the direct command which Christ gave us and the intimate link which baptism and eucharist have to Christ's work of the Reign of God.

Other sacramental actions are sometimes labelled "Sacraments of the Church," because the church recognizes them, through reflection upon the work of the incarnate Jesus and upon the Reign of God in the world, as particular ways in which God cultivates transformation in creation. Thus, some churches will add as many as five other sacraments to the list, including: confirmation, marriage, ordination, reconciliation, and anointing of the sick. Confirmation is a kind of fulfilment of the baptismal rite, in which people who were baptized very young (perhaps as babies) claim the promises made on their behalf and the church lays hands on them in order to share the Holy Spirit; the Spirit will empower them to live Christ's life.

Marriage is a commitment by two persons to live in unity and mutual love; the ring, or some such token, is considered to be the visible symbol. Ordination, in which a person is set aside to serve as a leader in the Christian community, includes a laying-on of hands, with a meaning similar to confirmation, though with a view to empowerment for leadership. Reconciliation, also known as "penance," involves a private and individual confession of wrongdoing toward God, usually said in the presence of an ordained person who will complete the action with a proclamation of God's love and forgiveness and the sign of the cross. In anointing of the sick, people in need of healing receive specially-blessed oil, usually on the forehead; they are reminded of God's loving concern and God's will that their lives be fulfilled in the best way. Such fulfilment is not necessarily the kind of healing that we would prefer; cancer is not always banished, injuries do not always disappear, and sometimes people die a physical death. Nonetheless, the sacrament of anointing often brings a kind of spiritual healing and peace that aids in physical healing or acceptance of suffering, whichever life brings.

All of life is sacramental, because God is transformatively present in and to everything. This is God at work, building up God's Reign. However, only those who participate in the church's sacraments are likely to be able to recognize the rest of life as sacramental and live it as such. The explicitly sacramental actions of the church have a life-changing effect upon the participants and, thereby, on everything else.

What is baptism?

Baptism is the sacrament through which people join the church. People being baptized receive water – they may have it poured on them or be fully immersed in it. Baptism is always done in the three-fold name of God – Father, Son and Holy Spirit. In some parts of the Christian church, a baptism that is not accompanied by the three-fold name is invalid; substitute forms of the name (such as the popular "Creator, Redeemer, Sanctifier", which is not really a Trinitarian form – see "Who is the Christian God?") are ordinarily unacceptable for baptism.

Baptism is at the heart of Christianity. According to the Bible, Jesus himself told us to do it. Jesus was baptized by a Jewish preacher, called John the Baptist. In turn, Jesus told his disciples to continue the practice. The oldest texts from the ancient church emphasize its importance. We have evidence of how it was done, both in written form and in the baptismal equipment remaining (such as the baptistry at The Church of St. John Lateran, in Rome).

Different Christian denominations vary on many things; on baptism, however, there is a limited range of variation. Some pour the water over the head, while others insist on a full entry into the water (flowing water is preferred by some of these people). The most significant difference, though, has to do with the age at which people are baptized. Some Christians baptize babies. These people emphasize God's faithfulness to the church and God's ability to act in people's lives even when we cannot fully understand how God is at work. This view emphasizes God's transforming activity in the world. Other Christians will baptize only adults, insisting that baptism is a sign to God of our willingness to follow Christ, which means that only people of a responsible age (usually at least mid-teens) may be baptized. This approach focuses on our response to God, and encourages people to be aware of the cost of following God's will. In either case, baptism is accompanied by commitments – both on the side of the congregation and on the side of the person being baptized (sponsors make promises on behalf of babies). We will discuss these commitments further on.

The real question which most people seem to face about baptism is: "Why bother?" You can live without it. You can even attend, and participate in, church without it (some churches no longer require that you be baptized before participating in the eucharist or occupying leadership positions). Baptism does not confer much in the way of obvious benefits; it certainly will not make you rich. Where is the value in it?

Part of the answer is found in our discussion about membership in the church (see "Why join the church?"). If you have decided to consider yourself a member of the church and wish to fulfil the church's membership expectations, then you will want to participate in the entrance ceremony. Such an answer does not quite resolve our dilemma, however, because it fails to explain why the church baptizes people and has traditionally required baptism as a condition of membership.

We are called to baptize by Jesus the Christ. The biblical texts trace the practice to Jesus's example, as well as his explicit command. At the beginning of his ministry, Jesus approaches John the Baptist with a request for baptism in the River Jordan (Matthew 3:13–17; Mark 1:12–13; Luke 3:21–22; John 1:29–34). John baulks at the idea, recognizing his cousin Jesus as the Messiah, the prophet and leader of the Reign of God for whom John is merely a precursor; the recognition is clear in Matthew's Gospel, but most vivid and developed in John's Gospel. Jesus insists upon the rite and is baptized. While the baptism is occurring, John the Baptist, at least, is aware of the Father declaring that Jesus is the Son of God. The Holy Spirit descends upon Jesus "like a dove."

This story has several features which help us to understand Christian baptism. Baptism, as administered by John, was a rite of purification and a declaration of intent to live a pure life. One of the reasons for the use of water in baptism is precisely that it symbolizes washing; it is the primary means by which people make themselves clean of the dirt and grime which we get on ourselves as an ordinary part of life in the world. People went to John for a ritual washing: they wanted to be cleansed of their sins and declare their intention to live differently. That is why John wants to refuse baptism to Jesus. John declares that Jesus should be baptizing him! Though he is already pure and in need of no cleansing, Jesus insists that John go ahead with the rite. Jesus's baptism is a declaration of his absolute commitment to his divine mission; which is the true meaning of purity. Commonly, we think of purity as being defined by our sexuality, vocabulary, diet or drinking habits. All of these are relevant, but only insofar as they reflect the degree to which we are focused upon the tasks which God has given us.

In this action undertaken by Jesus, we see an example for ourselves. For us, baptism is a washing-away of stains on our characters, created by prior misdeeds. However, this cleansing is not primarily directed toward the past. Instead, we are baptized to new life in Christ; the actions look forward to our participation in the Reign of God. Therefore, the focus of our commitment to purity is really a declaration that we accept the missions which God gives us and are prepared to work toward their fulfilment in the world.

While Jesus the Christ is being baptized, the Father announces the association between Father and Son. As Matthew describes the scene, "a voice from heaven said, "This is my Son, the Beloved, with whom I am well pleased" (3:17). This is a declaration of Jesus's participation in God; he is the Father's only Son, who shows the Father to the world. Similarly, in baptism the church proclaims our adoption into God's life, God's family. The church announces its recognition that we have chosen to live as children of God, as we announce our willingness to do so (or sponsors announce it for us). The church declares that it will stand with us and support us in our task of living in God's way. We are members of God's family and we have taken up the family business, living in God's Reign, living according to the divine plan which is the Father's gift.

We can know the Reign of God and live in it only because of the Holy Spirit's work. The Spirit gives us both knowledge and power. The visible manifestation of the Holy Spirit at Jesus's baptism reminds us that the Spirit is present at our own baptisms and will use them to form us as God's people. God's power is at work in baptism, which is an important reason why most Christians speak of baptism as a sacrament.

Immediately after being baptized, Jesus goes into the desert, facing forty days of testing and self-examination (Matthew 4:1–11; Mark 1:12–13; Luke 4:1–13). In response to specific challenges posed to him (the text has Satan or a devil speaking to him; I am inclined to think of this as the voice of temptation that resides in all of us), Jesus explicitly rejects apparent shortcuts to the Reign of God. He refuses to use power to feed the the world; he will not demand that the Father protect him from all harm, including the brutal death which faces him so soon in his ministry; he will not turn to evil in an effort to rule the earth. At our baptisms, we renounce any commitment to oppose God, whether because of allegiance to ourselves or to others. This includes an assertion that we are prepared to reject the forces of evil that show themselves in society. We declare that we will not give ourselves over to the ways of destructive power, even if those ways seem ultimately to serve some kind of good. Jesus's response to these challenges marks the beginning of his ministry. The same is true for us. Baptism occurs at the beginning of our lives as members of the church; it marks our commitment to God's way of being and acting in the world.

The baptisms that the church performs do not only mirror Jesus's baptism and immediately subsequent events. Our baptisms are also participations in the death and resurrection of Jesus the Christ. Water symbolizes the death of our old selves. This is most strongly evident in those traditions which completely immerse people in water: those being baptized go right under the surface, as if they were going down into the grave. Then they rise. The old life is dead; the new life begins. This is the new life which is given through Christ's resurrection; it is the victory over all death and destruction. Through the doorway of baptism, we enter into a taste of the Reign of God and look forward to the completion of God's Reign. This is the life to which Jesus calls us to baptize, in the name of the Father, Son and Holy Spirit (Matthew 28:19–20).

What is the eucharist?

We are only baptized once, but the great majority of Christians participate in the eucharist weekly and nearly all Christians have such a service more than once a year. In a sense, the eucharist is the meal that sustains us in our new life in Christ. The service is modelled on the Passover supper which Jesus shared with his disciples prior to his death. Christians take Jesus's actions and words at that supper very seriously.

Ordinarily, a eucharistic service will begin with Bible readings and a sermon. The readings draw us into the Christian story, while the sermon calls our attention to ways in which we can (indeed, must) live out that story today. Most Christians follow the sermon with a declaration of their faith in God, usually by reciting one of the ancient creeds. Then, we pray for the needs of the world and our own needs, as well as giving thanks for the blessings which we have received. At some point in this process, we confess to God that we recognize our failures to live in perfect relationship with

God and our neighbours. The worship leader (a priest, for most Christians; a designated leader, in some Protestant churches) proclaims God's forgiveness.

A "passing of the peace" often follows; this is an opportunity to greet other people with a blessing, because we need to be reconciled with our neighbours, as well as with God. Some people are inclined to pass the peace only with those whom they know and like. The priorities ought to be different: those with whom one is at odds and any newcomers always come first. They are the people who need to know that we wish to live with them in God's love. Our dearest friends already know this.

The specifically eucharistic action begins now. Since the publication of Dom Gregory Dix's *The Shape of the Liturgy* (London: A & C Black, 1945), nearly all Christians have recognized that their eucharistic services have a four-fold shape, modelled on the abovementioned supper which Jesus shared with his followers; Jesus *took* the bread, *blessed* it, *broke* it, and *gave* it to his disciples – and treated the wine similarly (only the bread is broken, of course). The bread and wine (or grape juice, for a few Christians) are taken and placed on the altar (some use the term "communion table," instead of altar). A prayer follows, including an account of salvation history – the story of God's salvific work from creation, through the people of Israel, to the work of Jesus the Christ. The eucharistic leader thanks God for the bread and wine and quotes Jesus's words: "Take, eat; this is my body," with reference to the bread, and "Drink from it all of you; for this is my blood of the covenant, which is poured out for many for the forgiveness of sins," with reference to the wine (Matthew 26:26–29; see also: Mark 14:22–26; Luke 22:14–23; 1 Corinthians 11:23–26). The leader breaks the bread. The bread and wine are shared with the whole community.

Christians have a long history of disagreement over what the bread and wine are; do these elements somehow take on a unity with Jesus the Christ which makes them, in some literal sense, Christ's body? Every position imaginable has been taken on this question. Some people, at one end of the continuum of arguments, insist that the bread and wine simply help us to remember what Jesus did. At the other end of the spectrum are those who tell stories about biting into the bread and having blood spurt out. Probably both of these extremes, the mundane and the gruesome, are too physicalist; neither can imagine aspects of reality other than the purely concrete, so that powerful symbols have no meaning for them. If the bread and wine are, indeed, visible and effective symbols of Christ's work in us and the world (a sacrament), then they are Christ's body. Any weaker assertion robs the symbols of their capacity to change the world; any stronger or more complex statement leads into the realm of unhelpfully speculative metaphysics.

Incidentally, some readers may be familiar with the Roman Catholic language of "transubstantiation." For those people, I will add that "transubstantiation" (as understood by Thomas Aquinas) is nothing more than the assertion that the bread and wine remain just that in every physical characteristic and behaviour ("accidents," in Aristotle's language), so that when they are eaten, the bread and wine taste and act as bread and wine. The change which occurs is in their power and meaning, because God has taken them over and given them a sacramental nature (the Aristotelian "essence"). The bread and wine become God's sacramental tools.

In spite of lengthy and painful debates about what happens to the bread and wine, the great majority of Christians agree on the working of the sacrament. The Body of Christ, the church, meets together. This is a sacramental action, announcing the presence of God's Reign and participating in that Reign. Christ is proclaimed, through reading of Scripture and through preaching; this shows forth the presence of the Word of God (Jesus the Christ) through the Bible and the preacher. This, too is sacramental, a visible participation in God's Reign. Elements of the physical universe, in which Christ is eternally present, are consumed – another sacramental participation in God's Reign. The church is then sent out into the world to be sacrament, finding and serving Christ in the world. Those in need are Christ to us – "And the king will answer them, 'Truly I tell you, just as you did it to one of the least of these who are members of my family, you did it to me" (Matthew 25:40). Thus, by participating in the Reign of God, we help others to know God's Reign.

In the one sacrament of the eucharist, we see many sacraments juxtaposed. This is the nature of the world. God is present in and to everything, through the Son, by whom all is brought into being. The universal nature of sacrament is demonstrated by the way in which sacrament meets sacrament.

The effectiveness of sacraments is also evident in the eucharist. People, including many who would not otherwise associate with one another, meet together to share a meal. They encounter the story of God's transforming love, the salvific work of the Trinity. Then, in the "passing of the peace," those same people declare their willingness to live in love and harmony with their neighbours – even those who irk them most. Eating the meal, the people become one body – Christ's body. At the conclusion, they are sent out in the power of the Holy Spirit, to live redemptively in the world, serving the Father's will in their own walks of life. Thus, the community is formed and transformed, so that the world is transformed. In partial and halting – but very real – ways, the Reign of God is shown forth in the congregation and everywhere.

The implications of the eucharist are cosmic. This meal is the decisive formative experience for the Christian community in its ongoing life. We ignore the practice and its meanings at our peril. We attend to the eucharist and its consequences to our eternal gain. However, the benefits are not solely to the individual, because benefits accrue to the individual only insofar as they are shared with the whole community of creation. The eucharist is a centre of power because God gives it power. However, it is only known by humanity as such a centre because it transforms lives. If we let the eucharist change us, then we will live in a closer and more intimate realtionship with God. We will also live in a more truly loving relationship with all of God's creatures. We become sacrament to God's creation; we become the Body of Christ. As we show forth the Reign of God, there is a kind of ripple effect. We live as sacrament and, thereby, enable others to live out the Reign of God more fully, which enables others to live out the Reign of God more fully, and so on, and so on . . . The eucharist is the heart of Christian life.

What are icons and why do people use them?

Icons are relatively new to most Western Christians, but they are a truly ancient part of Eastern Christian spirituality. Icons are pictures of a sort, although they are also much more, as we shall see. They are often found in small sizes – sometimes in frames – so that they are portable, but huge ones also exist. Size is important, because icons are an important part of the prayer and worship life of many people. Large ones adorn most surfaces of Eastern Christian churches, while small ones travel in purse or pocket.

To the untrained eye, an icon is merely a picture, done in a stylized and evidently symbolic way. However, an icon is really much more than that. Icons are similar to sacraments, because they are visible objects through which God works. The specific characteristic of an icon, however, is that it is usually a representation of God or a saint and a means by which the presence of the one shown on the icon is recognized. That is a tangled way of saying that an icon of St. Peter is understood to be the presence of St. Peter; we may show respect to him and ask him to share in our lives through his icon. The icon is a sort of window, through which we may enter into the world of the whole church, past, present and future, and through which the whole church enters our time and place. This is one of the most effective ways of experiencing the eternal that human creativity has devised, which is why Eastern Christians have traditionally emphasized the power of God's inspiration in the development of icons. God is seen as having directed the original birth of iconography, as well as the work of any particular iconographer composing any particular icon.

The practice of composing icons is called "writing," rather than drawing or painting. One writes an icon of the Holy Trinity. This is because an icon has the capacity to communicate meanings intended by the Word of God, the second person of the Trinity, whom we meet in Jesus the Christ. If we approach it prayerfully, an icon can draw us into the Reign of God. Simultaneously, that same icon can be used by God to establish God's Reign in and around us. Thus, we are drawn into the life of Christ, in communion with the Father and the Spirit. As a consequence of such an encounter, we can be empowered to go forth and live Christ's life in the world. The effect of life with icons is exactly parallel to life with other sacraments; icons are sacraments of a particular kind.

The "making-present" effect which we discussed earlier, combined with the activity of the Divine Word, explains the various behaviours which Eastern Christians, especially, undertake in relation to icons. Icons are objects of reverence, not because of their value as items made of wood, silver, gold and precious jewels – this is not idolatry – but because they are windows that open into the Divine Presence and the larger community which shares in the life of the Divine Presence. Icons hold places of honour in homes and other buildings. They receive affectionate and reverent attentions, such as kisses, expressions of love, and declarations of regret. Most of all, people pray and worship with icons and through them, sometimes speaking directly to God and sometimes addressing other honoured Christians with requests for guidance or intercession.

The true centre of life with icons is the church building. An Eastern Christian church will ordinarily have icons everywhere, because the true nature of creation is laid bare. One's feet are still firmly planted on earth, but one is made aware of living in the presence of the heavenly. Notable Christians (saints) from every part of history surround one, as do biblical figures. The four evangelists (Matthew, Mark, Luke and John) commonly appear at the top of four corners or pillars. Icons representing persons of the Trinity may be anywhere – sometimes everywhere – but there will almost certainly be a set above the altar, often on the ceiling. To reach the altar, however, priest and deacon must pass through a screen, called an *iconostasis*. The *iconostasis* serves two major symbolic functions: (1) it preserves the holy space around the altar, identifying it as truly part of another world (the *iconostasis* carries resonances of the entry into the Holy of Holies in the Jewish temple, as well as the Gates of Heaven); and (2) it announces that we have access to the holiest place, the Divine Presence, through the icons which cover it and through the three (Triune) doors which open at the appropriate, sacramental, times.

The modern age has met the sort of practices that surround icons with extreme scepticism. However, the world is slowly returning to such ancient expressions of devotion. We have a growing awareness of the limitations of empiricism (the belief that only the physically measurable is real). We are becoming aware of the need to recognize the numinous, that which causes things to happen but is not easily explicable. Icons remind us that God is eternal; God is present in and to every aspect of creation simultaneously. Icons also remind us that those who live in the presence of the eternal God, though they cannot be fully eternal, are able to transcend time and space through the power of love. This is true for creatures on both sides of an icon – saints from two millennia ago are present to our time and we can be present to theirs.

"Iconology" is a method of doing theology that is based in the study of icons. Protestants have a tendency to start from the Bible, while Roman Catholics often begin with the church and its sacramental life. Eastern Christians often start with the church (especially the early church – the first eight centuries) and icons. These approaches can be complementary, because they are built around the Triune God's self-revelation and work in history. All of them orient the attentive listener to God's Word, Jesus the Christ, and the transformative activity of the Trinity in our time, as well as other times. All three approaches help us to know the Reign of God.

The contribution of icons to life in the Reign of God is significant; it is a measure of their value to Christian life. In fact, icons have much to offer, especially to people raised in empiricist and individualist traditions of the modern world. Icons remind us that God is present in and to everything which happens in all of creation. God will not be banished from God's world, even if we attempt to shut our eyes to God's presence. Far better to strive for awareness of God's activity and live in an intimate relationship with God. Moreover, icons function as a visible link with people of all places and times who strive to be faithful. These people help us to be loving and strong in our own world, while reminding us of the limitations which are always attached to being human. Icons enable us to live in communion with God and God's people, living God's life in the world today. They are a visible and effective symbol of God's creative, redemptive and sanctifying activity in creation.

Why do we celebrate the Christian year?

The Christian year begins with Advent (in December), followed by Christmas, Epiphany, Lent, Easter and Pentecost. Taken together, these seasons amount to a whole year, though they begin and end at different times from the secular year. At our house, we have a New Year's Eve celebration prior to the start of Advent; it is a whole lot of fun (I recommend the idea!), but it does tend to confuse people. On the other hand, it emphasizes to the world that something else is going on in the story of life. That, really, is the point of the Christian year: the created order is more about what God is doing than it is about what we are doing – and what we are doing only has meaning in relation to what God is doing. The Christian year is about salvation history: God building God's Reign.

The first thing to remember about the Christian year is that it is sacramental. In other words, it does not merely remind us that there is more to creation than seems obvious. Instead, the Christian year calls us and enables us to participate in that other dimension of our reality. It helps us to recognize and live in heaven, rather than simply telling us that heaven exists.

The Christian calendar helps us to participate in the salvation that the Triune God gives to us. Advent is the first season; it includes the four Sundays before Christmas, so that the actual number of days in the season may vary. The word "Advent" is from the Latin for "coming" (*Adventus*): it is the season when we look forward to the coming of Jesus the Christ. It is meant to be a quiet, reflective time, when we live on our hope in God. We think about the meaning of Christian hope. Hope, for us, is a sure expectation of the transformation of creation which happens in the coming of Jesus the Christ. Consequently, we focus both on the coming celebration of the birth of Jesus and on the kingdom which that birth inaugurates. We prepare ourselves for the Reign of God by looking for signs of God's action and seeking opportunities to act as agents of God's Reign. This requires a still watchfulness. The contemporary festive season before Christmas can make this attitude difficult to achieve. On the other hand, all of the insanity of the pre-Christmas frenzy provides more than the usual number of opportunities to live the divine life. Today, Advent truly reflects another reality behind the apparent story of life.

Churches tend to decorate in either purple or blue for Advent. Purple is the traditional colour, because it emphasizes self-examination and penitence. At one time, many people used Advent as a time for cleansing, even fasting on occasion. The point was to prepare oneself for the coming Christ. Deep blue has replaced purple in many churches. The primary reason for the blue is that it emphasizes the kind of peaceful and calm reflectiveness which is suited to Advent. It is, however, more celebratory than the purple, which is now kept for Lent. The blue that we use is the colour of a deep and darkening evening sky, which focuses our thoughts toward the angels and star which announce the coming of the Christ child. This colour also reminds us of the light blue which is often used to help us celebrate the life of Mary, the mother of Jesus.

Advent is followed by Christmas. The Christmas season lasts for twelve days, beginning on December 25. This comes as a surprise to many people. Even those who remember the old carol about "the twelve days of Christmas" tend not to recognize that the 25th is the first of those twelve, rather than the last. Installing Christmas decorations in Advent and removing them at the very beginning of the Christmas season is liturgically awkward, at best!

Christmas is the celebration of the Incarnation. This is the time when we celebrate the union of God and humanity in the birth of Jesus the Christ. The liturgical colour is white, reminding us of the purity and innocence of the Christ child, as well as the glory of God shown in and through him. This is a season of pure joy. Remembering and participating in God's generous gift of life in Christ, many Christians share presents with each other and the world (some Christians focus upon the role of St. Nicholas and give gifts on or before the Feast of St. Nicholas, December 6). The practice of gift-giving has become intensely commercial. Everyone has picked it up, which is good, and greed has become a dominant characteristic, which is bad. However, Christians have always found other ways to give at Christmas, providing clothes, food and money to those in need. Many people will recognize this as the season for the Salvation Army's regular appeal, seeking money to support shelters for the homeless. The Incarnation establishes God's universal Reign on earth, with all of the implications which we have seen (see "What is the kingdom of God?" and all of our discussions about God) for justice and the common good. In Christmas season, we celebrate the Reign of God by going out of our way to perform special, symbolic actions which show that Reign. Thus, Christmas is known as a season intended for love, joy, peace and unending generosity (though, as is the way with life, our impulse to destroy creeps in all too often).

The next season, Epiphany, begins with another reminder that our wealth belongs to God, rather than us. On the twelfth night of the Christmas season, we celebrate the coming of the Magi to see Jesus. We do not really know much about these men, who appear only in the Gospel of Matthew (2:1–12). In the story, they show up in Jerusalem, seeking the newborn King of the Jews, because they had observed a star rising. Herod, ruler of Judea, hears of their coming and consults with the chief priests and scribes. On the advice he receives, Herod directs the Magi to Bethlehem, instructing them to return to him and tell him of the new king's whereabouts. Herod claims to desire a chance to bow before the new king, but secretly intends his death. The Magi find the baby, bow before him, and give gifts of gold, frankincense and myrrh. Following a dream-warning, the Magi leave by another road, evading Herod. After their departure, an angel appears to Joseph, warning him to take Mary and the baby and escape to Egypt. Joseph does so and the family survives.

The season of Epiphany calls us to reflect on a variety of different aspects of life in God; its central meanings can be found in the narrative of the Magi, a richly evocative story. Epiphany is, first and foremost, about seeing. An "epiphany' is a "manifestation" or an "appearance," something which is seen. The Magi begin by seeing a star, a visible sign of God's activity through the natural world, that will bring them to the Christ child. In other words, they start their journey to meet God by way of a sacrament, just as we do. Then, the Magi see kingship in a newborn baby, in humble circumstances, reminding us – simultaneously – of the uniqueness of Jesus the Christ and also that we may meet him in the most unlikely places.

Matthew speaks of the Magi as "wise men from the East." In Matthew's Gospel, the first people to worship Jesus are not Jews, though Jesus's ministry will be preoccupied with reaching Jewish people – and Matthew's text emphasizes Jesus as the fulfilment of Hebrew prophecy. The beginning of the story is, thus, linked to its conclusion, at which time Jesus will tell his followers to go and make disciples "of all nations, baptizing them in the name of the Father and of the Son and of the Holy Ghost" (28:16). The season of Epiphany continues the focus upon inclusiveness that is a consequence of the Incarnation. Jesus the Christ is for all people.

The gifts that the Magi bring are of peculiar significance. They function as reminders of the story of Jesus's life. Gold is the simplest: it is a kingly gift, a declaration that the things of the earth are in the hands of this child. Frankincense is a resin which is burnt during prayer, emphasizing the communion with the Father which characterizes Jesus's life. Myrrh is an ointment used in Jewish burial arrangements, linking Jesus's birth to his death. Epiphany makes us look upward, in a metaphorical sense, by causing us to look for the signs of God's work in the world. It also causes us to look forward toward the ministry of Christ and the death to which that ministry leads.

Another significant event in Epiphany is the celebration of the baptism of Christ. We have already discussed Jesus's baptism at some length (see "What is baptism?"). The Epiphany context, though, is important because it ties together many of the Epiphany themes. Baptism is a sacrament in which we see God at work. We do not have a star to follow, but we have sacraments that perform the same function for us. Moreover, baptism is a means by which we enter into the whole of Christ's life. It is our gift of ourselves to God and our symbolic participation in Jesus the Christ's life, death and resurrection. For some Christians, the Feast of the Baptism of Christ is the pivotal event in the season of Epiphany.

The liturgical colour for Epiphany is green, which is a sort of fallback colour in the church year. I am not aware of any particular aspect of the meaning of Epiphany that is emphasized by the use of green.

After Epiphany comes Lent, a season of preparation and fore-boding, even though its name is drawn from the cheerful lengthening of days which becomes evident during the February-March lenten time. Lent begins with Ash Wednesday, when many Christians have ashes put on their foreheads in a cross-shape, as a sign of repentance for the wrongs which we have committed. The season lasts forty days, mirroring the period which Jesus spent in the desert, fasting and being tempted (Matthew 4:1–11; Mark 1:12; Luke 4:1–13). Christians use Lent to reflect upon their lives and the ways in which the Reign of God is shown (or not shown) through them. Some Christians undertake special disciplines in Lent, fasting for periods of time and avoiding meat through the whole forty days. Often, people choose to forgo a specific pleasure, in order to focus more precisely on the world and its needs. Consequently, Lent can be a very important time of discernment, when Christians discover ways in which they can serve God.

Lent concludes with Holy Week, the most solemn period in the church year. Holy Week begins on an upbeat note, with Jesus's triumphal entry into Jerusalem (celebrated on a Sunday, known as Palm Sunday). However, immediately following this we begin to remember the events leading to his death. Some people attend special services in the early days of Holy Week, watching Jesus's progress. The experience intensifies on Maundy Thursday, when Christians gather to remember the Passover supper which Jesus shared with his disciples before his death. Some Christians share a meal, modelled after the Passover, as a way of participating in Jesus's meal with his disciples. Commonly, we ceremonially wash one another's feet at the Maundy Thursday service, as a way of entering into Jesus's action as he washed his disciples's feet and declared that true rulership is found in service to others. The next day is Good Friday, when we follow Jesus's journey to death. Some Christians meet for a "Stations of the Cross" service, in which we (symbolically) go step-by-step through Jesus's con-demnation, walk to the place of execution, time spent hanging on the cross, and burial. Astute observers will note that most "Stations of the Cross" outlines follow the Bible story, but add various pieces from traditional accounts of what happened. Good Friday is a solemn day, generally spent in prayer and fasting. Holy Saturday follows; it is a quiet, watchful, in-between sort of day.

The liturgical colour for Lent is purple, reminding us of Jesus's kingship, shown through testing, servanthood and suffering. In addition to causing us to reflect upon the meaning of true kingship, purple assists in forming a solemn mood. It encourages us to be penitent, thinking about the ways in which our lives do not reflect the Reign of God.

Then comes Easter! Easter is the joyous celebration of Christ's resurrection.

It begins after sundown on Holy Saturday, just like Christmas starts on Christmas Eve. Many Christians hold an "Easter Vigil," which traditionally occupied most of the night, but now usually lasts 2–3 hours. The service begins in darkness – the emptiness of Holy Saturday. Then a new fire is kindled at the entryway to the church building. From it, the Easter candle (called the "Paschal Candle") is lit. It is carried to the front of the church. Then, a hymn of joy (called the "Exsultet") is sung. A series of Scripture readings, selected from the whole of the Bible, follows, and a sermon may be preached or time may be left for reflection. Thus, we enter into the story of God's work in the world as Christians have always told it – starting with the creation of the universe; moving through the history of the Hebrew people to the Incarnation of Jesus the Christ, his birth, life, death and resurrection; and completing with the Holy Spirit's creation of the church and our place in God's Reign.

Baptisms may follow. This was the usual time for baptisms in the early church; ordinarily Lent would have been used as a time of fasting and preparation for baptismal candidates (today, churches often emphasize some form of fasting and study during Lent, as an echo of this practice). Easter is a marvellous time to be baptized, because of the wonderful way in which baptism picks up all of the symbolism of Christ's death and resurrection. For the same reasons, confirmations often occur during the Vigil. The whole community renews its baptismal vows, in concert with people receiving baptism and confirmation. The service concludes with Easter Communion, a eucharist which is central to the church's life. This celebration of the resurrection is one of the richest moments of the church year, a time when we truly feel the joy of new life.

Some Christians, especially from Protestant heritages, celebrate the coming of Easter with a "Sunrise Service" on Sunday morning. These services lack the strict, traditional form of an Easter Vigil, which can make them uplifting and lighthearted exercises of spontaneous joy. Such services often draw people from a variety of Christian traditions, celebrating Easter together. Participants rise early, with services commonly beginning around 7:00 AM, or just before dawn. In the quiet of Easter Sunday morning, hymns and prayers fill the air. "Christ is risen. The Lord is risen, indeed."

Easter lasts forty-nine days. In that time, the church is dressed in white, as a celebration of new life – and of the purity which is found in true faithfulness and commitment to the resurrected life. New life is the central theme of Easter; we focus upon Christ's eternal life, which he shares with us. Easter is a season of intimacy with Christ and with the world around us. We are reminded that the Reign of God is here, in and around us. Moreover, Easter occurs, for those of us in the Northern Hemisphere, as spring is taking hold of the world, so that we have a kind of visible trans-formation in creation reflecting the Easter story; this, of course, does not hold for our Christian family in Equatorial and Southern parts of the earth.

The fiftieth day after Easter is Pentecost ("Pentecost" literally means "fiftieth day" and is derived from a Jewish feast of the same name). At Pentecost, we celebrate the work of the Holy Spirit, remembering the day on which the Spirit transformed the disciples in Jerusalem (see "Who is the Holy Spirit?") and observing the Spirit's work in us and the whole world. On the feast of Pentecost, we decorate the church in red – and many churches really dec-orate, with red balloons, tongues of fire, and other reminders of the Holy Spirit's activity. Red is a colour used for many of the church's special celebrations, but it is particularly suited to the Day of Pentecost.

Pentecost is the longest season, lasting from sometime in May or June to sometime in November or December. In many churches,

Trinity Sunday is celebrated on the second Sunday in Pentecost; this is an opportunity to summarize the liturgical events that have already occurred and look forward to the rest of the year. In a sense, Trinity Sunday is the centre of the Christian calendar. It looks backward to Pentecost Sunday and to the seasons of the Incarnation, asking us to remember that the actions of the Holy Spirit and the Son celebrated at these times are in accord with the direction of the Father. It looks forward to the rest of Pentecost, which will emphasize the role of the church acting under the guidance of the Holy Spirit, while reminding us that these are rooted in the work of Christ and the Father. In other words, Trinity Sunday celebrates the work of the Trinity which is at the heart of Christianity.

Because Pentecost focuses upon the life of the church, it is our time; we do not so much enter into it as simply exist in it. Jesus the Christ is with the Father; we live in him and see him in a mystical sense, but do not walk with him in the absolutely literal sense of having the historical Jesus of Nazareth accompanying us down the street. Instead, the Holy Spirit moves in us, enabling us to live in Christ and see Christ in the world around us. We walk by faith, learning to listen to the Spirit's promptings and seeking to know and do the Father's will.

Sometimes, Pentecost seems endless. We wait for something dramatic to happen. The liturgical colour for the season of Pentecost is green, which is simply the ordinary colour and can come to appear boring. Then, one day, we realize that green is a colour of life and growth, a creative colour. We rediscover the sacramental joy of the Reign of God in ordinary things and are reminded of our work of living creatively in God's creation. We realize that plain is not so plain, and God takes delight in everything that God makes, even that which appears to be unexciting on the surface. We have found the richness of Pentecost.

Then, Advent takes us by surprise again . . .

The Problem of Evil

6

What is the good?

We often talk about good and evil as if everybody knows what they are – and anyone who differs from us is obviously on the side of evil. On the other hand, we sometimes insist that there really are no such things as good and evil; there are only individual preferences, lived out in particular cultural and historical contexts. Most of us know, however, that life is less clear than either of these simple theories suggest. In fact, there are some things that are evidently wrong. We recognize genocide, the wholesale slaughter of people simply because of their ethnic identity, as altogether wrong. I have not seen anyone attempt a reasonable defence of such an action; instead, perpetrators tend to deny that genocide is occurring or simply ignore criticism entirely. On the other hand, many of the questions that we face daily are not so easily labelled one way or the other, which is why we sometimes fall into the simplistic language of individual preferences.

Take the use of plastics, for instance. Most plastics decay at an extremely slow rate, so that we have massive landfills full of more-or-less permanent plastic objects which have no evident use. They pollute our oceans and endanger the lives of birds and sea-creatures. Moreover, while they are in use, they tend to affect the substance which they hold, so that food products packed in plastic will sometimes take on a "plasticky" flavour and will deposit residual quantities of plastic in the human body. On the other hand, I am typing this on a computer made largely of plastics, while staring through plastic "glasses." I have just been out running errands in my car, which contains a large quantity of plastic, some of it in the safety systems (seatbelts, airbags, etc.). Plastics are integral to most of the objects which we use today, including many of the things necessary for our health care system. We would not want to dispense with plastics – not really.

So what should we do? We can ignore the problem, which is what most of us do, most of the time. This unfortunately, is a time- and benefit-limited option. Landfills reach capacity and we need to find other places to put rubbish. The petroleum base that is used to create most plastics becomes more difficult to find and extract, increasing the economic and environmental costs involved. Consequently, we must seek a better alternative, which is to try to understand the problem and decide what the good is, in the circumstances which we face.

The first thing to be said, from a Christian perspective, is that the Bible is only indirectly helpful in the face of such an ethical dilemma. For Christians, the basic purpose of the Bible is to aid us in understanding God's work of salvation in the world; Scripture tells us who God is and how God is working with us (see "How should we read the Bible?"). That does not mean that the Bible will provide us with clear answers to such questions as whether/ how we should use plastics. Ethical decisions are not as simple as reading the Bible and finding the answer.

On the other hand, the Bible does provide us with some principles for making ethical decisions. The people who put together the Bible opted to begin with a creation story, found in Genesis 1:1–2:4a. That story reminds us that God makes all things and regards them as intrinsically good. That which God makes is, by definition, good! All of creation, then, is worthy of being loved and cared for.

The Genesis story tells us something else. It asserts that God makes us in God's image. What do we know of God when we are told this? Simply that God creates. That's it. That's all that has been said. To be made in God's image, then, is to be made as a creator. Performing this act of creation, God asks us to participate in God's creative work. The story ends with God calling upon us to share in the task of caring for the world. We are made to live creatively, caring for all things, and we must do so or die.

So, part of the answer lies in human creativity, exercised with a sincere love and concern for finding the best ways to live with and in the world. This means that we must try to choose the greater good over the lesser. By this, I mean that irresponsible use of plastic might be profitable, in the short term. Thus, such a course of action can bring good – more money in the pocket of a producer, for instance, that can be reinvested or spent in a way which brings more goods of various kinds to the producer. This is the choice of the lesser good, because it does not include consideration for the common good. The planet and other people will suffer because of this poor choice, as the producer will, ultimately. A degraded environment is destructive of the quality of life that everyone enjoys. The greater good, then, means always being attentive to the needs of other people and of all creation, as well as the needs which we have.

We must, therefore, be attentive, reasonable and responsible in our use of plastics. A sincere commitment to the simple formula, "Reduce, Reuse, Recycle," is a basic starting point. Christians ought to be in the forefront of efforts to build a sustainable economy, in part by identifying and living according to appropriate uses of plastics. Considering the needs of the world is important.

I realize that this does not sound particularly different from what any environmentally-aware person would suggest. There is no reason that it should. The good is the same for a non-Christian as it is for a Christian, while both are equally susceptible to self-deception.

The real difference between Christian ethics and non-Christian ethics has to do with the hope that Christians possess. The word "hope" here does not imply the degree of doubt that it is often taken to include. Instead, the word "certainty" might express the idea more clearly. At the heart of Christian belief is the assertion that God is, in Christ, reconciling all things to Godself. Being an environmentally-concerned person can be a depressing business. The quantity and variety of destruction which is part of human living escapes any effort at measurement. Each and every week, the newspaper seems to provide new evidence of the complexity of the created order and the ways in which we mess it up. Toiling away at the job of helping humanity to become aware of its dangers and finding ways to improve the situation can take the heart out of the most irrepressible optimist. True Christians know that they must contribute to this effort; such work is part of their God-given task. We also know, however, that God is acting redemptively in the world. Death will not triumph. Thus, having done their best all day, Christians can go to sleep at night in trust that God holds all of heaven and earth in divine care, which exceeds all human imagining. The Reign of God is the final answer; my work is not.

The good, then, is the Reign of God, which means living according to God's will. We do this when we live creatively, making the most of the talents and inclinations which God gives us, and when we focus upon that which serves all of creation. We must take the broad and long view, which gives consideration to all creatures now and in the past and future, while remembering that the future is in God's creating, redeeming and sanctifying "hands."

What is evil?

We have discussed the good. In some ways that was easy, because we all know something about what sorts of things are good for us and the world. But what is evil?

This question is complicated, because all things in the world are good, by nature. They are good because existing is a good and all things serve good purposes. This is a result of their origins: God makes them and uses them for God's purposes. Nothing that God makes can be, in itself, evil.

"Fair enough," I hear you say, "but what of Adolf Hitler and the Holocaust, or Mao Tse-Tung and The Great Leap Forward? What of child abuse and crystal meth, of people caught in apparently endless downward spirals of violence, poverty, destruction? What, in short, are we to make of the ugly side of life?"

Indeed, ugliness is visible. We must not avert our eyes. Surely, that, if anything, is a biblical command. The call of the prophets is always to care for the hopeless, helpless and needy. Jesus heals the leper and calls upon us to offer the cup of water to the thirsty. We see evil, and its presence is a puzzle that troubles and confuses all of us. What sort of thing is evil?

Perhaps the most important point to understand is that evil is not a *thing*. God does not make it. It has no existence of its own. It is not even a necessary quality of anything. There is not a thing in existence which is evil, as such. Instead, evil is a hole where a good should be. It is an absence.

When a person commits a murder, many evils are involved. Love that ought to be in the murderer is absent. The proper relationship between the person who murders and the victim is absent, because the two are not relating in the right way. The murderer could have been doing good things; those good things do not happen. The victim had all kinds of life possibilities which have suddenly vanished. These are all absences; they represent unfulfilled potential for good.

What are we to make of the passions which drive people to murder? These passions are usually (perhaps *always*) desires for peace or freedom or money – all of which are good things, in themselves. The problem is that the murderer has chosen to pursue a good in a way which destroys much more than it creates. The murderer has chosen the lesser good over the greater. The murderer's desire for a particular good has become disordered; that desire has taken priority over considerations that ought to have been more important. The murderer's primary goal is desired out of right proportion to other 'goods' in that person's life. Consequently, the murderer is not living rightly and is failing to fulfil the potential which God has given that person.

Ultimately, evil offers nobody any real benefit. Evildoers may obtain the goods that they seek. However, they have traded life and meaning for those goods, by choosing the lesser goods. That is, first and foremost, because evil choices form evil character. Habitually making evil choices leads to perennial dissatisfaction, for the goods that one receives are never the best that one ought to receive. Moreover, the desire for them is not a healthy desire and is unlikely to be satisfied with what it gets.

An obvious example of such evil training is a desire for sweet foods. They are a good, for our bodies need some sugar and fat. However, we do not need much of these things. If we pursue sweets, refusing protein (meats, eggs, dairy and legumes) and vitamin-rich foods (fruits and vegetables), neglecting to take in fibre and complex carbohydrates (whole-grain breads, for example), then we find ourselves overtaken by desire for sugar. Our bodies are not satisfied with a sweet diet, so that we demand more of it. We become diabetics and obese. We are well on the way to self-destruction; only the most intrusive measures (regular insulin treatments, for example) can save our bodies from death.

Destroying things is part of our life; indeed, very nearly all of our creative activities are associated with some act of destruction. At lunch today, I destroyed a piece of fish. However, we need to choose carefully what we create and what we destroy. This may be the greatest lesson to be learned from the environmental movement: we need to take care in our treatment of the creation around us, for what we do to it will affect what it does to us. Breaking it will break us. In other words, the wrong decision is evil because of the possibilities that it eliminates. We create absences where God's good things ought to be and we are among those good things.

Evil is the spirit of destruction. It is being so concerned about ourselves and our desires that we are prepared to destroy things that should not be destroyed. It is having no gratitude for what we receive and always seeking more, however "more" might be defined in our lives. We are not called to live this way. Indeed, we are not designed to live this way.

Instead, we are called to live in the spirit of creativity, which is a spirit of love. This is true life, given by the Holy Spirit. Instead of working to destroy people, creatures and the earth, we must seek to help them live in the Reign of God, as much as we possibly can. Our job is to seek the common good, to care for all as best we can. We must cultivate a spirit of generosity and gratitude, rather than focusing upon our public status or our possessions.

What is original sin?

The doctrine of original sin is in bad odour these days. Nobody wants to talk about it. Sometimes, this is because it has fallen prey to some rather strange theories about what original sin is and how it is communicated. More commonly, though, we ignore this doctrine because it says some ugly things about the ways in which we behave and the consequences of our actions.

"Sin" has two meanings: (1) the intentional commitment of a destructive action, and (2) the intentional failure to undertake a constructive action. As the Apostle Paul says, "I do not do the good I want, but the evil I do not want is what I do" (Romans 7:19). We see opportunities to show God's Reign by accomplishing something creative; yet we choose not to act. We see opportunities to do something destructive and act immediately.

Every sin which we commit has implications for those around us and those who follow us. In the second creation story (Genesis 2:4b–3:24), Adam and Eve choose the particular path of development which we all take. They sin, acting out of pride and desire for control. By sinning, they come to know good and evil, empirically. One consequence of their sin is that other people, including their children, are hurt. The earth is damaged. Everything becomes more difficult, less pleasant. Selfishness comes into play and people begin to know shortages. The cycle goes on. This is original sin: the sin that becomes part of the world's life. Original sin becomes a part of the context in which children are formed from birth; it gets passed on – often in ways that we do not even notice.

Original sin is part of life, as we know it. Right now, the world is in an uproar as it discovers that our indiscriminate release of pollutants into our environment is contributing to global warming, a rapid increase in temperatures affecting the air, water and earth. We look back on two centuries of industrial development, undertaken with little more than a nod (if that) to environmental consequences. As things stand, North Americans live in vast houses and drive huge, toxin- and greenhouse-gas–releasing automobiles. We have seen the benefits of acting without a thought for the rest of humanity or the created order. Now, we begin to see the price tag. The payments are coming due.

This is an empirical demonstration of the doctrine of original sin. The doctrine of original sin says nothing obscure or even complicated. We all know its meaning and implications, because we live it every day. Evil done today begets evil tomorrow.

At times, the power of sin appears to be overwhelming. We take a step back, look at the world and shake our heads in fear and horror. Deliverance seems impossible. The power of original sin is precisely what makes the gospel of God's redemptive work so important. God redeems, even when we do not realize it. However, the possibility of true hope is contingent upon the reconciling work of the Triune God. We know that God reigns and will reign. We know that doing the good is meaningful, because God uses our work to break the cycle of original sin. Each of us can be a channel of blessing to our own place and time, defeating the powers of destruction and participating in the triumph of life.

Some readers will be familiar with an account of original sin according to which the body is held responsible. Sin is understood to be an aspect of the human body, passed down genetically from a first ancestor. This is a faulty and dangerous theory. It is faulty because physical stuff cannot sin; it has no capacity to decide, for good or evil, and cannot be held responsible for sinful actions. By itself, a body cannot form an intention to do evil or avoid doing that which is good. Mind and body must work in concert, because the mind gathers information, understands it, judges the accuracy of its understanding, and makes decisions. Only under rather unusual circumstances – such as an adverse reaction to medication taken in good faith, for example – are we willing to say that a person's mind played no part in an action. The material stuff of which we are made cannot, reasonably, be held responsible for our decisions. The body influences our choices, but does not make them.

The idea that original sin is a characteristic of the human body is dangerous because it tends to breed dislike, sometimes hatred, of bodies and of physical life. Sexual life is frowned upon. Bodily needs take second place to spiritual needs, so that feeding the hungry is less of a priority than preaching to them. The focus is upon a spiritual life with God, that is often understood as really beginning after death – when the body can no longer interfere.

This attitude is a kind of Gnosticism. Gnosticism is a heresy which has pursued the church from its very early days. Its adherents seek a kind of spiritual existence, because they believe physical stuff to be intrinsically evil. Gnostics cannot really accept the humanity of Jesus the Christ, because the Incarnation implies that God values the material world. Instead, their emphasis is always upon Jesus as divine. To Gnostics, Jesus's humanity consists solely of a body, used as a sort of camouflage. Christ is not understood as ushering in the Reign of God on earth; instead, he enables us to escape the physical realm for life in a heaven that is completely separate from the material universe. Some of the original Gnostics insisted that creation is a product of an evil creator, rather than the good God. However, many others reach the same theology by arguing that the good God created the universe, but sin has placed it under the total control of Satan/the Devil/evil powers (see: "What is the Devil?"). Either way, the goodness of creation and the power of the Incarnation are both denied – and our bodies come to be seen as fundamentally evil.

Gnosticism is neither Christian nor helpful; hatred of God's creation is sinful and the cause of great evil. Original sin is much more accurately understood as a characteristic of social life. We inherit sin through education: when I make wrong choices, my children learn to make wrong choices We form other people to make sinful decisions and develop destructive habits. Blaming our bodies will not relieve us of the task of learning and teaching good ways to live.

What is the Devil?

Everybody has a mental picture of "the Devil." Usually, the picture is humorous, a cartoon with flames, a red pitchfork, and horns sticking out of his head. Ardent readers might think of a debonair gentleman, inclined toward practical jokes. Whatever the picture, the Devil goes around doing everything that is evil and nothing that is good. The shorthand definition of the Devil is "the personification of evil;" evil made visible in the form of a person.

That definition is simply impossible. Evil cannot be made visible in a physical form. If evil appears in the form of a person, then that person must immediately commit suicide. Otherwise, there would be an evil that the evil one had not committed – the evil of self-destruction. In other words, by allowing himself to live, the Devil would be doing something good – avoiding an evil.

Evil is an absence, an emptiness where a good should be. If evil is to be visible, then good must be present also. Good exists. Evil is simply the destruction of good things or good possibilities. When we do evil, we destroy good things and eliminate good possibilities, including possibilities within ourselves. However, our selves remain the creations of a good God who is eternal and knows all ends. Besides, we always have the possibility of doing good. One cannot be purely evil if one has the possibility of doing good, even if that good only serves oneself.

Positing an evil being who need not do all evils but functions as an evil encouragement to others, pushing everyone else to do evil, does not resolve the problem. Such a creature need not commit suicide. However, doing evil is always destructive of the self; it cannot be otherwise. Maintaining any sort of character through a succession of billions of evil decisions is an unimaginable impossibility.

Besides, all of those evil decisions will have been good for somebody, somehow. Evil consists in choosing the lesser good over the greater good. Dumping toxic chemicals into a river, in order to avoid the cost of proper disposal, is an evil thing to do. Still, the dumper obtains some benefit, a good, in the form of reduced business costs. Temptation works in precisely this way. We are attracted by some sort of good, while ignoring the destructive consequences of the desired course of action. To sustain our picture of a devil, then, we need to design it as a creature that can always distinguish the lesser good from the greater and push us to accomplish just that much good. This is how the artistic picture of a devil who adopts a debonair, smooth and pleasant façade comes into being. Such a devil is no more feasible than one who does all evil. After many, many choices of the lesser good over the greater, no creature can be attractive – or even know what an attractive appearance might be. This Devil is, however, more helpful symbolically, because it captures the nature of temptation more accurately.

True forces of evil are the social manifestations of original sin. The pressure that we feel to engage in a destructive pattern of behaviour, even when we know it to be destructive, is evil. When marketers set out to create a hunger for their products, knowing them to be unhelpful or second-rate, then the marketers become the generators of evil. Cigarette companies, lacing their cigarettes with extra nicotine to enhance addictive power, have worked in this way. Personifying evil can, itself, be a dangerous strategy because it tends to obscure the real origins of temptation. A devil is not merely theologically unnecessary and philosophically impossible, it is also ethically unhelpful. Blaming some sort of malign force of the universe undermines our commitment to social criticism, while hiding from our eyes our own inclinations to respond to social forces.

In Bible stories, we encounter a variety of figures who seem to be evil powers of an inhuman sort, though fewer and less often than people tend to think. Often, our conversations about the power of evil owe more to extra-biblical traditions – John Milton's poetry, for example – than to the Bible itself. What are we to do, though, about these biblical references to "devils" and "Satan" and malign forces?

We must remember that we are not automatically required to believe everything that ancient people believed, even if it appears in the Bible (see "How should we read the Bible?"). The church selected and continually returns to the biblical documents because they tell the story of God's creative, redeeming and sanctifying work. This is the decisive point which was brought out by the early church councils. They emphasized the scriptural ideas about God and salvation that we need to understand and believe. We need not accept the physics, geography, cosmology or any other aspect of the ancient world's thought-systems.

Moreover, careful scrutiny of the biblical texts suggests the presence of more complex thought about personifications of evil than we commonly expect. "Satan" appears as the force of opposition to God; his name means "adversary" (from Greek: *satanas*). Satan is understood, for much of the biblical period, as a being with personality. While he does, in some sense, oppose God, God always holds the reins. In the Book of Job, Satan appears as a kind of stock character, supporting a lengthy theological discussion about innocent suffering. Job is written almost entirely in poetry and seems to be a play, with Satan playing a cameo role. At God's permission, Satan causes Job to suffer as a test of Job's faithfulness to God. God is in firm control of Satan, establishing the conditions of Satan's work and turning it to God's own purposes. In Luke's Gospel, Jesus declares that he has seen Satan fall from heaven (Luke 10:18). This may be a statement about a particular being, although Jesus's words have a poetic and metaphorical sound to them. Whatever Jesus means by "Satan," the thrust of his statement is that Satan is powerless against Jesus and his followers. God is fully in control. Even the Book of Revelation, where material about Satan is most in evidence, focuses upon his downfall and imprisonment.

An intriguing episode appears in one of the stories about Jesus (Matthew 16:21–28; Mark 8:31–38). Peter, one of Jesus's followers, wants to protect Jesus from the horrible death that awaits him. Jesus gets angry at Peter and calls him "Satan," because Peter is preventing Jesus from fulfilling his mission. "Get behind me, Satan! For you are setting your mind not on divine things but on human things" (Mark 8:33). Jesus goes on to emphasize that we must be prepared to lay down our lives, if we are really to live. Jesus's comment to Peter seems to imply two things about Satan: (1) focusing on human inclinations, rather than God's purposes, is the essence of being satanic; and (2) we can be Satan, by opposing God's work in the world. If we make ourselves and our own desires into ultimate values, then we become God's adversary.

Belief in a supernatural being that opposes God seems to be untenable and unnecessary. If, however, one holds to ancient traditions and persists in the belief, then one must also accept the biblical conclusion that God is firmly in control of that being and turns all of its works into good. Whichever position we take, we must remember that we can participate in the forces which oppose God's will. Such forces will not ultimately triumph; God redeems all things for the Reign of God. However, we can be tremendously destructive to ourselves and others when we opt to be the adversary.

Can there be a just war?

If destruction is evil, can the ultimate act of destruction – war – be justified?

This is a question which is always fresh and immediate, I am sad to say. There is always a new war to be faced and whenever a war happens, we see again the useless waste and destruction of this most unholy manifestation of human power. We are forced to ask, not merely about the legitimacy of this particular war, but also of war, as such. At the core of Christianity is Jesus the Christ, who told Peter to drop his sword (John 18:10), and went to death willingly instead of reordering all of creation to prevent this evil thing (Matthew 27:53–54). Indeed, rebuking the one who used the sword (only John tells us that it was Peter), Jesus said, "Put your sword back into its place; for all who take the sword will perish by the sword" (Matthew 26:52). As we have seen ("Why did Jesus die?"), this willingness to die for the world is connected to the vision of the Reign of God, in which there will be no more violence and the wolf will be at peace with the lamb (Isaiah 11:6). Are we not called upon to live in this vision of peace, prepared to give up our lives to avoid a fight?

Certainly, some Christians have taken this position. Most North Americans and Europeans have some familiarity with strains of Anabaptist (believers in adult baptism) Christianity that are firmly pacifist, such as the Amish and traditional Mennonites. They point to biblical references like the ones I've mentioned, insisting that only love should be shown to everyone and emphasizing Jesus's own example of non-resistance. Commonly, they also turn to the example of the early church, which strongly discouraged Christians from entering military service. Such Anabaptist groups often have a firm commitment to caring for others; here, in Canada, the work of the Mennonite Central Committee in alleviating suffering and assisting others in difficult times (regardless of the beliefs of those who suffer) is legendary. However, they insist upon following Jesus's example of standing up for the weak, while avoiding any act of violence. On this position, there is no justification for taking the life of another person and cutting off the possibilities of divine redemption and growth in this life for that person.

The majority of Christians, however, have adopted a different stance, maintaining that there are some circumstances which demand a violent response, even including killing. Most Christians would insist that violence is destructive and, therefore, normally unacceptable. However, the Western Christian tradition has developed a set of criteria, usually called "just war theory," as a means to help in deciding whether going to war might be appropriate. It was first stated by Thomas Aquinas, who insists that three things are necessary for a war to be regarded as just: (1) a legally constituted, national government must make the decision; (2) the opponent must have done something wrong, of the sort which makes war an appropriate recourse; and (3) the nations responding with war must have rightful intentions, "so that they intend the advancement of good, or the avoidance of evil."[1]

The first requirement may seem unfair to some. After all, what is a group of people who do not believe themselves to be justly represented in the sovereign state to do? Thomas's answer is that such people must seek legal redress through the ordinary processes of justice within the state. This is a good answer, as far as it goes, because it focuses upon the need to avoid feuds and other internecine battles. Turning to violence is often an easier reponse to injustice than the long, drawn-out process of seeking change through courts or governmental institutions. Violence, though, can be the choice of despair, and it rarely produces the kind of results for which people hope. Violent means rarely lead to peaceful and just conclusions; in principle, it is very difficult for them to do so, because violent action begets violent response in a cycle which is not easily ended. In addition, healing afterward is a

---

1. Thomas Aquinas, *Summa Theologica* (Westminster, MD: Christian Classics, 1981), IIa IIae Q. 40, a. 1; 3. 1353–1354.

time-consuming and delicate process. Non-violent change is usually more thorough and permanent; sometimes it is also quicker, precisely because it tends not to breed the same, deep-rooted thirst for vengeance and redress.

National structures have evident shortcomings. They are often based upon highly artificial boundaries, imposed as a consequence of all sorts of political influences which have little relationship to political, social or topographical geography. Notions of justice and the means by which it is to be obtained vary from country to country. Unfortunately, perfect justice is not to be found anywhere. Some systems are better, some worse (and some, *much* worse), but all have limitations.

However, nation-states are our received structures; they are what we have for duly-constituted, legal authorities. Consequently, working through them to make decisions about war is reasonable. Most matters which justify war occur at the national or international level, anyway, and that is the level at which diplomatic efforts to avoid war can be made. The just war theory is generally correct to insist that wars must be legally declared by national governments.

Nonetheless, there is one question left outstanding: "What of cases where national governments undertake wholesale policies of slaughter, genocidal or otherwise, within their own borders?" The first answer, of course, is that other nations have a duty to intervene. Whether they do or not, however, internal war is justified on such grounds. Fighting Pol Pot, Mao Tse Tong, Adolf Hitler, Josef Stalin or other such butchers is perfectly legitimate; indeed, it would seem to be morally imperative. Where the lives of millions of innocent people are at stake, then taking the lives of murderers is just.

This brings us to the issue of causes of war. The most traditional justification for war is that "Country A" has crossed the boundaries of "Country B," without sufficient reason. Because this is organized theft and is usually accompanied by murder, rape and other violent actions, such boundary-crossing is ordinarily deemed to be just cause for Country B to declare war on Country A and resist violently. This is one of the more complicated issues in Christian ethics, however, because those who hold to an absolute prohibition on violence criticize the principle of self-defence. They argue that Christians have no right to self-defence, since the fundamental principle of Christian life is self-giving, in accordance with Jesus's example.

In contrast, others insist that there are limits to self-giving, which are established by one's tasks in life. Jesus's mission was partly fulfilled in his violent death, while many of us would have our missions destroyed by such a premature end. On this argument, we have a limited right to self-defence, which must be exercised in proportion to the actions taken against us.

Still others have argued that Christians have no right to self-defence, but that the work of a soldier in a just war hardly constitutes self-defence. Such a person often runs a much greater risk of personal harm than civilians living beyond the limits of the war-zone. On this argument, the work of a soldier (done properly) must be seen as self-sacrifice for the defence of others and is, therefore, appropriate for Christians. These latter views have generally prevailed in the eyes of most Christians.

Earlier, we alluded to another just cause of war, which is the behaviour of ruling authorities within a nation-state. This is a part of the theory which is in the early stages of development; it has been used in a number of cases in recent years: Somalia, Afghanistan, Iraq. The argument is that the government in place in Country B is so violently repressive in its treatment of its own population that intervention by Country A is justified. On the principle of defence of others, this can be a solid argument. National borders are not so impermeable that the world community ought to stand by helplessly, while observing mass genocide.

Nonetheless, the use of this justification has forced us to be even more aware of Thomas's third requirement for a just war: right intention (which must be sustained throughout the war). In other words, humanitarian intervention – or any other reason for fighting – must not be used as a pretext for the fulfilment of other, less savoury, goals. If a war becomes an opportunity to grab land, power, natural resources or any other benefit, then it has immediately ceased to be just. Self-defence must remain defence of self; defence of others, whether in one's own country or elsewhere, must remain defence of others. Under no circumstances may a war of aggression be regarded as just, according to this theory.

At the root of just war theory is the belief that better ways must be found to fulfil human needs. Violence is a last resort, to which we are sometimes pushed by the unacceptable behaviour of others. It should not be undertaken with our own interests in view, but only with the intention of caring for the world and its needs. We look forward to the completion of God's Reign, when this whole conversation will end.

Conclusion: What is the gospel?

What is the gospel?

I meet many people who have given their lives to the church – worshipping, praying, listening to sermons, attending Christian education events, serving on committees, and trying to live out all that they learn in everything that they do ("the whole nine yards," as is said where I grew up) – but cannot state the Christian message in a short and simple way. That is reasonable enough. Christianity is complex; even a book as long as this one can hardly be said to have captured the whole story. Besides, most attempts at brief statements of the meaning of Christianity (such as the popular "Four Spiritual Laws") are dangerously simplistic and even false, losing much that is central to Christian understanding and life. People are wise to shy away from such unhelpful statements.

More in-depth treatment of Christian meaning is necessary. That is why I wrote this book; I have tried to make Christianity accessible to everyone from the interested but uninvolved through to the lifelong faithful. I hope that reading it has given you greater insight into the nature of Christianity and the reasons for its existence.

Nonetheless, there is still a need for a kind of summary statement that picks up the heart of the Christian message and may be shared when people are not likely to sit down and read a book. What answer can be given when someone asks, "What is the Christian gospel? What is the good news that justifies all of that church stuff?"

Here goes:

God – Father, Son, and Holy Spirit – brings everything into existence and helps all of it to grow into what God knows to be the best possible. "The best possible" means life in proper relationship to God. Thus, God is, in Christ, reconciling all things to Godself, through the activity of the Holy Spirit. We are invited to share in that work and participate in life with God, entering into the love which is at the root of all creation. We can see instances of God's Reign here and now; we know that God will complete God's Reign in us and in all things. Life in the Reign of God – in right relationship with God and all aspects of creation – is the life of true joy and peace.

There it is, folks. That is what I've tried to say in this book. If it seems as exciting to you as it is to me, then "Go tell it on the mountain, over the hills and everywhere."[1] Love shared is love squared. Ditto for joy and peace.

The peace of the Lord be always with you.

---

1. Words from a hymn by John W. Work, Jr., *Folk Songs of the American Negro* (Nashville, Tennessee: 1907).